THE COMING
Digital God

Virtually all Scripture references are quoted from the King James translation of the Holy Bible.

The Coming Digital God

Copyright ©2001 by Midnight Call Ministries
West Columbia, South Carolina 29170
Published by The Olive Press, a division of Midnight Call Ministries -
P.O. Box 280008, Columbia, SC 29228 U.S.A.

Copy typist:	Lynn Jeffcoat, Kathy Roland
Copy Editor:	Susanna Cancassi
Proofreaders:	Angie Peters, Susanna Cancassi
Layout/Design:	Michelle Kim
Lithography:	Simon Froese
Cover Design:	Michelle Kim

Library of Congress Cataloging-in-Publication Data

Froese, Arno - Froese, Joel - Brown, Jerry
  The Coming Digital God
  ISBN #0-937422-50-9

  1. Prophecy

Printed in the United States of America

CONTENTS

Chapter 7

THE BEAST, THE FALSE PROPHET AND THE MARK

• Who Is The Beast? • Evolution • No Laboratory Proof • Creation Is To Be Understood By Faith • Satanic Trinity • Why Is The Antichrist Called The Beast? • Satan's Origin • Equality To God • Modern Equality • Globalism And Equality • Christians And Globalism • You Can't Argue Success • The "You Are God" Deception • God Became Man, But Man Cannot Become God • The Antichrist's Power Of Deception

Chapter 8

THE "OTHER" BEAST

• Caution: Beast At Work • First Deception • Standing In Faith • How To Stand • Who Is The False Prophet? • A Lamb With Two Horns • Religion And Economy • Personality Cults • Power Of The False Prophet • Power Of Religion • Economic Globalism • Military • Media Success • Lying Signs And Wonders

Chapter 9

THE IMAGE

• What Is The Image Of The Beast? • The Authority Of The Image • Power Of Economy • Power Of Nationalism • The Two Prophets • Summary

Chapter 16

Chapter 17

Conclusion

"Take heed that no man deceive you" (Matthew 24:4).

The motivating factor behind writing this book can be summarized with one word, "truth!" To discover its meaning we are not required to study law, science, philosophy or theology. Absolute truth cannot be obtained through any of these channels regardless of how sincere or important it may be, because truth is not based on knowledge. Truth is based on a person, the One who said, *"...I am...the truth...."* Therefore, if truth is found in a person, then it stands to reason that falsity must also be embodied by someone. Jesus identified the lie, *"Ye are of your father the devil, and the lusts of your father ye will do. He was a murderer from the beginning, and abode not in the truth, because there is no truth in him. When he speaketh a lie, he speaketh of his own: for he is a liar, and the father of it"* (John 8:44).

Since it is a biblical fact that man is ruled by, and willingly follows the prince of darkness, who is the god of this world, it is quite natural that man is incapable of distinguishing truth from lies. Darkness and lies go hand-in-hand, just as truth and light are synonymous. Therefore, the primary reason for writing this book was not to shed light for those who are in darkness, but rather to shed some light on deception. The words, *"...Take heed that no man deceive you"* were not addressed to the world, but was Jesus' response to the disciples' question, *"...Tell us, when shall these things be? and what shall be the sign of thy coming, and of the end of the world?"* (Matthew 24:3).

Why would Jesus warn His followers about deception? Because deception appears as though it is truth. It looks real but is fake, and sounds right but is wrong. It is received as truth but in reality it is a lie.

Throughout these pages, I have attempted to demonstrate how the Bible teaches that peace and prosperity will cover the earth as never seen before, but will be built upon a lie. This lie is based on the foundation of success.

Our system of government, economy and finances are extremely successful. Historically, people have never been as wealthy as they are today. A simple laborer working on an assembly line in a factory has a supremely higher standard of living than any king, emperor or immensely rich man could have ever dreamed of just a few hundred years ago.

Success has conquered the elements. No longer do we shiver in the winter; today our offices, transportation and houses are heated at the touch of a button.

Success in communication is virtually mind-boggling. Years ago, letters sent from one continent to another took several months to reach their destination. A reply would take even longer. People who migrated to America could not attend the funeral of loved ones back in Europe because notice of death would have taken days, if not weeks. Additionally, the overwhelming majority were too poor to afford a trip to Europe.

I venture to say that the success we are now witnessing is only the tip of the iceberg. With each passing year, we are elevated to a higher level of comfort. But attached to that comfort, our dependence on the God of creation is diminishing. The phrase, *"...Give us this day our daily bread"* has become old-fashioned. Why? Because every nation in the world, with very few exceptions, has the capability of producing an abundance of food, primarily due to the introduction of the mechanized farming industry and the successful use of artificial pesticides and fertilizer.

However, this success does not depend on faith in a living God. The farmer who strives for success, works hard and follows the latest scientific methods in agriculture—regardless of where his faith lies—is the one who harvests the greatest crops. Therefore, it stands to reason that our descendants will become less dependent on God the Creator and will increasingly place their faith and trust in man's ability to chart the course of his own destiny.

After studying the Bible on a daily basis since 1967, it is my deep conviction that man's cleverness will direct him to a false god, the one Jesus warned His disciples about, *"...Take heed that no man deceive you."*

I have enlisted the help of Jerry Brown and Joel Froese, two experts in the electronic field who have each contributed a chapter to this book. This additional information about the world in which we live, as well as the direction our scientists are heading, is very revealing. It is important to add that all information outside of Scripture—particularly computer science which is growing at a phenomenal rate—is subject to change. But the direction toward man's self-achieved success is unquestionable. Consequently, our belief in the emergence of a digital god will prove itself to be true before too long. So I conclude this introduction with the passage of Scripture found in Revelation 13:11–18, "*...I beheld another beast coming up out of the earth; and he had two horns like a lamb, and he spake as a dragon. And he exerciseth all the power of the first beast before him, and causeth the earth and them which dwell therein to worship the first beast, whose deadly wound was healed. And he doeth great wonders, so that he maketh fire come down from heaven on the earth in the sight of men, And deceiveth them that dwell on the earth by the means of those miracles which he had power to do in the sight of the beast; saying to them that dwell on the earth, that they should make an image to the beast, which had the wound by a sword, and did live. And he had power to give life unto the image of the beast, that the image of the beast should both speak, and cause that as many as would not worship the image of the beast should be killed. And he causeth all, both small and great, rich and poor, free and bond, to receive a mark in their right hand, or in their foreheads: And that no man might buy or sell, save he that* *had the mark, or the name of the beast, or the number of his name. Here is wisdom. Let him that hath understanding count the number of the beast: for it is the number of a man; and his number is Six hundred threescore and six."*

Chapter 1

IDOLATRY VS. TRINITY

Documentation demonstrating the various means by which man has attempted to obtain the help of God exist in volume. In doing so, man has allowed his imagination free reign resulting in the production of all types of statues and images which were meant to symbolize or represent God. This is formally known as "idolatry."

Before Moses died he said, *"...ye have seen their abominations, and their idols, wood and stone, silver and gold, which were among them"* (Deuteronomy 29:17). In this verse we are clearly told that idols of any form are considered an abomination to God.

Approximately 800 years later, the prophet Habakkuk uttered this proclamation, *"What profiteth the graven image that the maker thereof hath graven it; the molten image, and a teacher of lies, that the maker of his work trusteth therein, to make dumb idols? Woe unto him that saith to the wood, Awake; to the dumb stone, Arise, it shall teach! Behold, it is laid over with gold and silver, and there is no breath at all in the midst of it"* (Habakkuk 2:18–19). The distinct difference between idols and the Living God is revealed in verse 20, *"But the LORD is in his holy temple: let all the earth keep silence before him."*

Some may say, "But that's from the Old Testament; that's ancient history!" That may be true, but we must remember that God's Word is eternal; past, present and future are immutably one. Virtually the same events taking place today will also occur in the future. We read the following words in Revelation 9:20, *"And the rest of the men which were not killed by these plagues yet repented not of the works of their hands, that they should not worship devils, and idols of gold, and silver, and brass, and stone, and of wood: which neither can see, nor hear, nor walk."* What was true in the beginning when, in his ignorance, man invented his own god, applies to our current day as well as the future.

THE STATE OF IDOLATRY

There's no need to detail how we can become guilty of worshipping idols today. Suffice it to say, modern-day idolatry exists in many different forms. For example, many of us no longer work to make a living; instead, we work to achieve a higher standard of luxury. The more we have, the more we want. Man is never satisfied with what he has; he always wants more.

This is particularly noticeable in today's global economy. Good is defined by statistics showing economic growth. If there is no growth, experts tell us that we are in a recession.

We are only satisfied when things continue to get better. If we could go back 50 or 60 years, we would notice how dramatically things have changed. There is absolutely no comparison between the beginning and end of the last century. People living in the early 1900s simply fought to survive. Today, our goal is to see how much luxury we can gain. The western world is particularly guilty of worshipping success. That behavior is known as "economic idolatry." Please keep that thought in mind because it is the key theme of this chapter.

SPIRITUAL IDOLATRY

Our greatest danger lies on the spiritual level. During my many years in ministry, I noticed that the most difficult times we have had in sending forth the precious Word of God was when the economy has been good, with low unemployment and high incomes. During bad times marked by high unemployment and soft economy, people seemed to become hungry for the Word of God, and were eager to support missionary outreach with generous assistance.

This is not unusual. Moses warned his people about prosperity, *"When thou hast eaten and art full, then thou shalt bless the LORD thy God for the good land which he hath given thee. Then thine heart be lifted up, and thou forget the LORD thy God, which brought thee forth out of the land of Egypt, from the house of bondage"* (Deuteronomy 8:10,14). Thus, we can rightly conclude that peace and prosperity present the greatest danger.

When times are bad, we cry out to God and beg for Him to intervene. However, when peace and prosperity prevail, we pride ourselves on the fact that we are masters of our own destiny. In order to understand man and the world in which he lives, we must analyze this matter from a biblical perspective.

Two key words—diversity and unity—will stand out in this chapter and should show us where we come from, where we are, and where we are going. To begin, let's talk about the God revealed to us in the Bible as the Father, Son, and Holy Spirit.

TRINITY

God's uniqueness is revealed in the Trinity. Although the actual word is not found in our Bible, we know from the context that a triune God is clearly taught.

As a matter of fact, the first three verses in our Bible clearly demonstrate God revealed in three persons:

GOD THE FATHER

"In the beginning God created the heaven and the earth" (verse 1).

GOD THE HOLY SPIRIT

"And the earth was without form, and void; and darkness was upon the face of the deep. And the Spirit of God moved upon the face of the waters" (verse 2).

GOD THE SON

"And God said, Let there be light: and there was light" (verse 3). When God speaks, it is the Word of God, the Word which became flesh. This is confirmed in John's gospel account: *"In the beginning was the Word, and the Word was with God, and the Word was God. The same was in the*

beginning with God. All things were made by him; and without him was not any thing made that was made" (John 1:1–3).

The first time God identifies Himself in a plural form is found when He created man in His image: *"And God said, Let us make man in our image, after our likeness "* (Genesis 1:26). Later in Genesis 11:7 when the people built the Tower of Babel we read, *"Go to, let us go down...."* Notice the use of the small word "us." Who was God talking to?

Can we describe the mysterious unity of God the Father, Son and Holy Spirit? Nobody can. Why not? Because our intellect is limited and is not capable of comprehending the eternal things of God.

Many who have attempted to explain, or explain away, the reality of the Trinity have stumbled and fallen. In cases where cults are concerned, the doctrine of the Trinity is rejected and branded as heretical! But this perfect unity, maintaining three distinct identities, is a fundamental doctrine taught in the Bible.

Jesus expressed this unity in His high priestly prayer in John 17:22–23, *"And the glory which thou gavest me I have given them; that they may be one, even as we are one: I in them, and thou in me, that they may be made perfect in one; and that the world may know that thou hast sent me, and hast loved them, as thou hast loved me."*

So we see that in order to understand God, we must first have a spiritual understanding of the Trinity.

TRINITY OF MAN

To the church at Thessalonica, the apostle Paul wrote, *"And the very God of peace sanctify you wholly; and I pray*

God your whole spirit and soul and body be preserved blameless unto the coming of our Lord Jesus Christ" (1st Thessalonians 5:23). From this text we see that man also consists of a trinity: spirit, soul, and body. The body comes from the earth and returns to the earth. The spirit comes from God and returns to God. The Bible says, *"Then shall the dust return to the earth as it was: and the spirit shall return unto God who gave it"* (Ecclesiastes 12:7). The soul connects the spirit and body. The "real" person is not the perishable body, but our spirit/soul. As believers in the Lord Jesus Christ, we are born again of His Spirit. We are in the presence of the Lord the moment we depart from our physical body. Why? Because the Bible says that, *"...flesh and blood shall not inherit the kingdom of God."* The transformation of the body takes place at the Rapture of the Church.

Unlike our body, neither our soul nor our spirit can be defined in medical terms. In other words, we can't ask our physician to remedy a problem of our soul or spirit. The soul and spirit escape the scalpel of a surgeon. In literature, the soul and spirit cannot be made subject even to the most prolific writer. The intellectual world is confronted with a mystery when it attempts to analyze the spirit and soul.

Medical science has made remarkable progress during the last few decades and has achieved near miraculous results with innovative procedures and amazing drugs; however, when it comes to the spirit and soul, medical science is silent.

Yet the Bible speaks so much about the soul. In the

King James translation, the word "soul" and "souls" appears approximately 536 times. In most cases, the word "soul" is used liberally. In fact, even when referring to the life of man the Bible uses the word "soul." The soul is an important part of man's body because *"...your whole spirit and soul and body be preserved blameless unto the coming of our Lord Jesus Christ."*

What then is the difference between spirit, soul, and body?

SPIRIT

The spirit of a believer is born of the Spirit of God. Our spirit has received the Spirit of God and, as a result, not only do we have assurance of our salvation for all eternity, but we also receive a guarantee of our inheritance, *"Which is the earnest of our inheritance until the redemption of the purchased possession, unto the praise of his glory"* (Ephesians 1:14). A person becomes a new creation when he is born again. Second Corinthians 5:17 states, *"Therefore, if any man be in Christ, he is a new creature: old things are passed away; behold, all things are become new."* Notice that the words *"...all things"* only relate to the new person. This does not include the body. When we read the entire context of that chapter, we see that under the inspiration of the Holy Spirit, Paul counts himself dead in Christ. *"...one died for all, then were all dead...henceforth know we no man after the flesh..."* (verses 14,16). Therefore, if we are *"...in Christ,"* then *"...all things have become new."*

The born again person's soul and body must now

become subject to the Holy Spirit, which is of God. This is every believer's greatest battle. It's not the bad situation we may find ourselves in, nor the wars we wage against crooked politicians, crime, or drug abuse; the most serious battle takes place when our trinity—spirit, soul and body—is in disharmony.

Many believers today, in the end stages of the endtimes, confuse the spirit and soul and find themselves in a losing fight against evil.

How can we maintain the victory? By heeding the words given to us in the Holy Scripture, *"For the word of God is quick, and powerful, and sharper than any twoedged sword, piercing even to the dividing asunder of soul and spirit, and of the joints and marrow, and is a discerner of the thoughts and intents of the heart"* (Hebrews 4:12). Notice that the Word of God divides the soul from the spirit. Based on that fact, a spiritual person will know whether he is led by the soul or the spirit.

SOUL

As I just mentioned, the soul and spirit are scientifically and medically unidentifiable; nevertheless, man has a soul. The soul must not be confused with the body. Unfortunately confusion is often the case when reading the Bible. Apparently the translators had a difficult time distinguishing between the life of a man in flesh and blood and the soul. What is the soul? The soul is the avenue by which we connect to the visible world, subjecting our soul to our flesh and blood. It is our soul that perceives joy and sadness. It also causes us to weep bitterly when disappointment or tragedy strikes. It exalts us to the heights of heaven when we experience happiness, prosperity, and well being. You might say that the soul is the throttle which controls our emotions. It is important to emphasize that what pertains to the soul must not be confused with what pertains to the spirit. This combination is often the cause of conflict within the Church of Jesus Christ. Many have experienced a conversion in their soul but it never led to the rebirth of the spirit.

Some will testify of amazing answers to prayer, even miracles such as the physical restoration of the body, but these things do not necessarily relate to the spirit and are not a confirmation of a spiritual rebirth.

A genuine rebirth of the spirit can be determined by the fruits of the Spirit listed in Galatians 5:22–23, *"But the fruit of the Spirit is love, joy, peace, longsuffering, gentleness, goodness, faith, meekness, temperance: against such there is no law."* Notice that it does not say "the fruit of the soul" but *"...the fruit of the Spirit."* If we keep these two important entities separate as they were intended, we will not be led to and fro by every wind of doctrine because we have become spiritual people who are reliant on the Word of God as our spiritual food.

BODY

The third part of the trinity of man is his body. Our soul pampers the body and agrees with its desires. As we have already seen, the spirit is the dividing factor in relation to the body. In Galatians 5:16–17 we read,

"...Walk in the Spirit, and ye shall not fulfil the lust of the flesh. For the flesh lusteth against the Spirit, and the Spirit against the flesh: and these are contrary the one to the other: so that ye cannot do the things that ye would." In this verse, we see that the flesh *"...lusteth against the spirit."* Here we are given the key to avoiding spiritual bankruptcy. The flesh always prides itself on being spiritual; it *"...lusteth against the spirit."* Yet the Bible says that the flesh has no promise: *"Flesh and blood shall not inherit the kingdom of God."* We are taken from the dust of the ground and that is where we shall return, unless the Rapture takes place first.

The description of the works of the flesh are also outlined in Galatians 5:19–21, *"Now the works of the flesh are manifest, which are these; Adultery, fornication, uncleanness, lasciviousness, idolatry, witchcraft, hatred, variance, emulations, wrath, strife, seditions, heresies, envyings, murders, drunkenness, revellings, and such like: of the which I tell you before, as I have also told you in time past, that they which do such things shall not inherit the kingdom of God."*

Therefore to understand man, we must first understand the trinity of man: spirit, soul and body.

Chapter 2

THE TRINITY OF THE HUMAN RACE

Fundamentally speaking, three primary races exist:
1. European
2. Asian
3. African

All other people, tribes or groups are related to these three races. The two remaining continents—America and Australia—are the result of European globalization.

The Bible lists Noah's three sons as Shem, Ham, and Japheth. When we follow the genealogy listed in Genesis 10, we can place Japheth, the youngest son, in Europe because the names of his sons are Gomer, Magog, Tubal, and Meshech.

Ham, the middle son, can be identified in an area such as Egypt, Sheba, or Dedan. The names of his sons can be traced to the south of Israel.

Shem, the oldest son, and the names of his descendants indicate the territory east of Israel, which is Asia.

Further research reveals that the descendants of Noah's sons overlap territories. I think it is virtually impossible to determine exactly which people came from where. What we do know is indisputable; the entire human race descends from Noah.

Summarizing Japheth's descendants we read, *"By these were the isles of the Gentiles divided in their lands; every one after his tongue, after their families, in their nations"* (Genesis 10:5). It is assumed that the shifting of the continents took place as recorded in verse 25, *"And unto Eber were born two sons: the name of one was Peleg; for in his days was the earth divided; and his brother's name was Joktan."* A number of theories exist in the field of geology, and all are attached with different conclusions showing how America and Australia were originally part of the big land mass of Europe, Asia and Africa.

Genesis 10:32 emphasizes the division of the nations after Noah's flood: *"These are the families of the sons of Noah, after their generations, in their nations: and by these were the nations divided in the earth after the flood."*

It is amazing to see the enormity of factual information provided us in the Bible. If you study anthropology, read the Bible. If your field is geography, read the Bible. This is a book given by God to man so that each of us may recognize that there is a God in heaven who has created all things and who has prepared a way for each of us to return to Him: through Jesus Christ. He declared, *"I am the way, the truth, and the life: no man cometh unto the Father, but by me"* (John 14:6).

GENTILES, JEWS, CHRISTIANS

A further trinity can be recognized within these three groups of people:

1. Gentiles
2. Jews
3. Christians

Prior to Abraham, all people were Gentiles. Through Abraham's seed, God chose a special people—later called Israel—for special purposes. Among those purposes is the call to be a light to the Gentiles. This is made clear in Isaiah 49 *"...Thou are my servant, O Israel, in whom I will be glorified...I will also give thee for a light to the Gentiles, that thou mayest be my salvation unto the end of the earth"* (verse 3 and 6). This was an unconditional promise. Israel's existence was not based on merit, but on God's eternal resolution. It is the Creator of heaven and earth who says, *"...I will."*

Although the world recognizes that the Jews are a unique and remarkable people who have kept their distinction from ancient times to modern civilization as leaders in philosophy, academics, art, science and technology, they have not yet fulfilled their original calling.

Moses made the following statement regarding Israel's future in Deuteronomy 15:6, *"For the LORD thy God blesseth thee, as he promised thee: and thou shalt lend unto many nations, but thou shalt not borrow; and thou shalt reign over many nations, but they shall not reign over thee."* This prophecy has not yet been fulfilled.

At this time, Israel is lending foreign aid and technical

know-how to many nations. However, as far as finances are concerned, Israel still has to borrow from other nations. And we can say with assurance that Israel does not *"...reign over many nations."* This will come to pass because it is another unconditional promise issued from the eternal ordinance, the Creator of heaven and earth.

SALVATION IS OF THE JEWS

Another significant reason for Israel's election is salvation. We just read that Israel's selection was based on God's intention to implement salvation worldwide. Jesus stated, *"...Salvation is of the Jews."* While this promise is fulfilled by Jesus' accomplished work and personal promise that He would build His Church, we recognize that a global fulfillment is to come.

The prophet Micah concludes his book with these words, *"He will turn again, he will have compassion upon us; he will subdue our iniquities; and thou wilt cast all their sins into the depths of the sea. Thou wilt perform the truth to Jacob, and the mercy to Abraham, which thou hast sworn unto our fathers from the days of old"* (Micah 7:19–20). Today, Israel's sins are very obvious, but the promise says that God *"...wilt cast all their sins into the depths of the sea."*

Has God's promise to Abraham, Isaac and Jacob been fulfilled? Let's read Genesis 28:14, *"...thy seed shall be as the dust of the earth, and thou shalt spread abroad to the west, and to the east, and to the north, and to the south: and in thee and in thy seed shall all the families of the earth be blessed."* We would be guilty of twisting Scripture if we said that this promise has been fulfilled by the Church.

Scripture plainly says, *"...all the families of the earth."*

Salvation doesn't only include the individual believer who comes to Jesus in repentance, asks forgiveness, and receives Him into his heart; but extends to Israel and the world. However, this fulfillment will only take place after God's severe judgment has come upon Israel and the nations.

The time will come when God pours out His compassion and love for His people so that promises such as Zephaniah 3:20 will be fulfilled, *"At that time will I bring you again, even in the time that I gather you: for I will make you a name and a praise among all people of the earth, when I turn back your captivity before your eyes, saith the LORD."*

CHRISTIANS

The third group of people we will examine are completely different from the previous two. They are not destined to be judged, nor have they received physical or geographical promises as did Israel. Christians are those who have accepted salvation from the Lord Jesus Christ.

According to Ephesians 5:32 the Church is a mystery: *"This is a great mystery: but I speak concerning Christ and the church."* That is why "Churchianity" and nominal Christians are at a loss when trying to identify the true Church. For that reason, religious "Churchianity" desperately tries to produce a unity that is supposed to show the rest of the world that they are the Church. This ecumenical tendency to organize unity among various denominations and churches is destined to fail because the mystery cannot be explained through any infrastructure. The Church of Jesus Christ is not subject to the pope in Rome or to different conventions and denominational headquarters; it is exclusively subject to its head: Jesus Christ.

GEOGRAPHIC LOCATION OF THE CHURCH

Gentile countries are defined by geographic borders which are recorded in many documents. The nations have numbered their citizens and know exactly how many people belong to their respective country. Each of those nations is administrated by a government that is usually located in one of its main cities. The government knows what is produced, what is earned and how much is owed. Gigantic bureaucratic systems function with the purpose of keeping up with the continuous change of each nation.

But these and other standards of measure do not apply to the Church. No one knows exactly where the Church is, nor the number of its members. It is not possible to determine the Church's wealth, acquire statistics documenting how many Christians have died, or equate how many were added to the Church yesterday. For these and many other reasons, the Church remains a "mystery."

Therefore, to define the Church we must look to the Lord, who explained, *"For where two or three are gathered together in my name, there am I in the midst of them"* (Matthew 18:20). The Church may be found in the most obscure places, but wherever believers are gathered.

Unfortunately, our culture has confused the Church of Jesus Christ with buildings and organizations. A church, by whatever name, can only be considered "the" Church when at least two or three born again believers have gathered in His Name. If no believers are found in a particular church, we may as well just call it a "supper club" or a "cultural society." It would not be wrong to use that facility as an entertainment center.

The Church, (i.e., her members) are scattered in every corner of the world. A recent statistic indicates that evangelical Christians in China make up 5% of the population. That is approximately 60 million souls! China has been "closed" to the Gospel, missionaries have been denied entrance, and Christian literature was forbidden to be imported, yet despite these obstacles, the Church of Jesus Christ is alive and well in this communist country. This is a wonderful confirmation of Jesus' promise to build His Church.

Chapter 3

POLITICAL TRINITY

Three major endtime political philosophies are:
1. Capitalism
2. Communism
3. Socialism

To better understand the world in which we live and to see the prophetic Word in various stages of fulfillment, it is important to analyze these three fundamental systems.

Capitalism can be defined in so many different ways because of the existence of so many different nations. Simply stated, capitalism is power over capital, which produces power over people.

Abraham was a capitalist. In his time, capitalism was primarily defined by how many animals and servants you owned.

In Genesis 13:6 we read, *"And the land was not able to bear them, that they might dwell together: for their substance was great, so that they could not dwell together."* Abraham and Lot owned so much capital collectively that they had to separate. Abraham gave Lot the first choice, *"Is not the whole land before thee? separate thyself, I pray thee, from me: if thou wilt take the left hand, then I will go to the right;*

or if thou depart to the right hand, then I will go to the left" (Genesis 13:9).

This separation was necessary for God to fulfill His promises to Abraham, whose seed the land of Canaan—from the Euphrates River to the river of Egypt—was given.

The 14th and 15th verse of this account is significant, *"And the LORD said unto Abram, after that Lot was separated from him, Lift up now thine eyes, and look from the place where thou art northward, and southward, and eastward, and westward: For all the land which thou seest, to thee will I give it, and to thy seed for ever."* Notice that God's promise to Abraham was fulfilled, *"...after that Lot was separated."*

Contained in these words is a spiritual message to believers: we have an obligation to God. When we are not attached to our surroundings, or, as in Abraham's case, family, (Lot) then God can speak to us individually and make His will personally known. If you feel rejected, isolated, or someone has done you wrong, then thank the Lord because He is getting ready to speak to you.

Lot chose the land in the area of Sodom and Gomorrah. Eventually, he found himself in a difficult situation and was taken captive by enemy forces. Everything he had was lost; another capitalist took away his capital.

How very fortunate for Lot that he had his uncle Abraham, a man who served the Living God. Not only did Abraham own a great herd of animals and servants, he also had a trained army. *"And when Abram heard that his brother was taken captive, he armed his trained servants, born in his own house, three hundred and eighteen, and pursued them unto Dan. And he divided himself against them, he and his servants, by night, and smote them, and pursued them unto Hobah, which is on the left hand of Damascus. And he brought back all the goods, and also brought again his brother Lot, and his goods, and the women also, and the people"* (Genesis 14:14–16).

POWER OF CAPITALISM

Stock and land-based capitalism continued over the next 4,000 years. The system varied from country to country, but the fundamentals stayed the same. Accumulated capital represented the economy and the financial system which was secured by military power. Power over these systems remained in the hands of the strongest leader.

Following history, we see that although many systems were implemented, capitalism's basic principles remained the same: the rights usually belonged to the strongest.

VOLUNTARY COMMUNISM

A brief intermission in capitalism took place in Jerusalem approximately 2,000 years ago. Believers established a system in which each member would have sufficiency in all things, whether rich or poor. Acts 4:32 reports, *"And the multitude of them that believed were of one heart and of one soul: neither said any of them that ought of the things which he possessed was his own; but they had all things in common."* It is important to point out that this first system of communism was voluntary.

When Ananias and Sapphira hypocritically held back part of the proceeds of the land they sold to the apostles for the Church for themselves, they were confronted by Peter who asked three questions in Acts 5:4:

1. *"Whiles it remained, was it not thine own?"*
2. *"...after it was sold, was it not thine own power?"*
3. *"...why has thou conceived this thing in thine heart?"*

This was a voluntarily surrender of capital for the well being of the Church so that a communistic system could be implemented.

No evidence in the gospels or prophets indicate that God ordained this new system so that all people would have all things in common. Based on Scripture it did not last.

However, capitalism continued as the prevailing system entrenched in virtually all countries of the world.

MODERN COMMUNISM

Although historic writers report of communal living in many parts of the world, the fundamentals of capitalism were never more seriously challenged until 1848 when Karl Marx and Friedrich Engels released their book, *The Communist Manifesto*.

Before we discuss communism, I would like to share my experiences with the system. I lost my place of birth because of communism. My family's roots date back 800 years to a town called Windenburg in East Prussia, but it can never be called "home" again. Accounts of the immense suffering my family experienced because of communism could fill a book. Even as recent as 1964, I had the frightful experience of being arrested in East Germany for trespassing the communists' "workers and farmers paradise" without a proper visa. Needless to say, I was happy they did not keep me in their "paradise."

It is important that when we analyze the truth, we should never base it on presuppositions, nationality, philosophy or experience. Therefore, we will dissect the philosophy of communism from as neutral a perspective as possible. We will also discuss some of communism's positive aspects as well as its contribution to today's social-capital-democracy.

History details many differences between various groups of people and their philosophies at different times. It cannot be argued that historically, those who had the power (force) also had the money (capital). Quite naturally, accumulated capital was passed from generation to generation forming a privileged class of people who became known as the *aristocracy*, a group believed to be superior to all others. The aristocrats inherited riches and power from their predecessors. Cultural development of any given form fell exclusively in the hands of this so-called "upper class."

It was not difficult to keep subjects in power during that time. The majority worked on farms and were at the mercy of the landowner who ruled the people. The workers, or peasants as they were called, depended upon the good will of their masters, the capitalists, to provide them with food, clothing and shelter. So whenever a power struggle arose, the peasants virtually always found themselves on the losing end while the upper class had the lower class tightly in its grip.

EUROPE BEFORE MARX

Up until the late 1800s, higher education in Europe was reserved solely for the upper class. The average family was grateful when a son was accepted as an apprentice in a local craft. Because the economy primarily revolved around agriculture, a much larger portion of the population lived in small villages and towns throughout the land. The mayor, councilmen, law enforcement, teachers, religious leaders and local businessmen controlled the town. Although steam-driven trains connected large cities, the average person had to walk in most areas. In order to own a horse and buggy two things were necessary: space to park and land for the horse to graze. Since most of the land was in the hands of the local landowners, it was very rare for the average person to own such luxuries.

THE GREAT CHANGE

A great number of Europeans migrated to North and South America and Australia during those days. The United States and Canada held the greatest attraction for central and northern Europeans because the climates were similar. Central and South American countries such as Spain and Portugal were more attractive to southern Europeans.

Those people who arrived in the beginning and middle of the 1800's experienced extreme hardship. Basic human rights, or workers rights, barely existed. Most people worked between 60–80 hours a week just to make a living. Children as young as 11 years old were expected to help support their family. It was certainly not unusual to find children employed in coal mines, road construction, farms, or iron works. They were grateful to have jobs and earn a dollar.

The Industrial Revolution gained visibility throughout Europe and the Americas in the 1800s. With less people working on farms and more working in the industry, the cry for change was natural.

Meanwhile, many wars had been fought. During those times, tremendous progress in the invention and manufacture of machinery was being made. The lower class, who were no longer satisfied with just getting by, began their search for a larger piece of the pie. Volumes of material report the uprisings of the lower class against the upper class during this time.

MARXISM

Karl Marx was one of the most successful philosophers in the middle of the 1800s. Coupled with Friedrich Engels they masterfully summarized the condition of the lower class, comparing it with the upper class in the book, *The Communist Manifesto* released in 1848, giving birth to modern communism.

The early struggle between capitalism and communism became evident during 1917, when the communist revolution began with the intention of taking over the Russian government by force. Since that day, capitalism and communism grew to the point where they diametrically opposed one another. This was highlighted by the communist Soviet Union in the east and the ever-expanding power of capitalism led by the United States of America in the west.

World War I solidified communist rule over Russia and World War II made Russia the undisputed winner by adding most of eastern Europe into the fold of communism.

The People's Republic of China emerged in September 1949, four years after the end of World War II. With an immense arms build-up on both sides, many analysts predicted that war was inevitable. Communism proved to be the stronger camp, rebellions were crushed, and the communists did not yield one inch of territory.

To hold the advance of communism in Asia, the French set up a government in Vietnam which was opposed by communist leader Ho Chi-Minh. The French recognized the impossibility of the situation and withdrew, making room for the United States to venture into a confrontation with the communists.

The loss of the Vietnam War, especially on a moral level devastated the United States. For the first time, it seemed as though communism would triumph globally. However, we all know the end of the story. Soviet communism could not succeed even in it's own territory. One item was lacking: religion. Not one nation has ever existed for any length of time without religion. While there are many other reasons to explain the collapse of communism, religion was certainly a great contributor.

Another major factor was its insistence on not accommodating change. Again, *The Communist Manifesto*, with Lenin's interpretation, had become the communists' "Bible," but did not accommodate the changes wrought by the Industrial Revolution. One could argue that communism had been beneficial for the 1800s, but was outdated by the 1900s. Communism fell and bankruptcy became an embarrassing reality in the late 1980s. However, as we will see later on, capitalism continued to change with each new wave of development in Europe and the rest of the world.

NATIONALISM

During the early years of conflict, another system known as "national-socialism" arose. This new political philosophy wedged itself between communism and capitalism. National-socialism aimed to nationalize all services required for the well being of all citizens and promised peace and prosperity. Adolf Hitler tried to eliminate communism in the east and opposed capitalism from the west. National-socialism flourished during the first 6 years of his rulership, but the following 6 years were marked by bitter catastrophe: World War II! This ended the political and economic philosophy of national socialism; however, it was not the end of socialism.

There is little disagreement over the fact that communism dug its own grave. The fate of the Soviet Union was sealed with the fall of the Berlin Wall—the most visible symbol of the division between capitalism and communism.

DEATH OF CAPITALISM TO COME?

We would be mistaken to assume that capitalism is alive and well and that communism and socialism have died. Before we define the death of capitalism, lets take a look at what the Bible says about the future of the Gentile nations.

All Bible readers are familiar with the second chapter of Daniel in which the four Gentile superpowers (Babylon, Persia, Greece and Rome) are described. The end of these superpowers is documented in verse 45: *"Forasmuch as thou sawest that the stone was cut out of the mountain without hands, and that it brake in pieces the iron, the brass, the clay, the silver, and the gold; the great God hath made known to the king what shall come to pass hereafter: and the dream is certain, and the interpretation thereof sure."* This stone—the Lord Jesus Christ cut out of the "mountain" which is the Mount of God—not only destroyed the iron and clay, but the brass, silver and gold as well. In other words, the statue, representing all the nations, will continue to exist until the very end when together, they will be destroyed. This verse clearly reveals that neither the gold, silver, or brass disappeared before the final destruction of the iron and clay. You can't destroy something that does not exist; therefore, it should come as no surprise that Iran (Persia) and Iraq (Babylon) are in the headlines today!

CAPITALISM TODAY

When analyzing today's capitalism, we find that in its historic sense, it no longer exists. In order to recognize the difference, we need to compare America when it was founded in 1776 to America today.

What type of capitalism prevailed during the founding of the United States? The one who owned the capital, usually defined in the form of land, was in charge. For instance, after the Constitution was ratified, a capitalist form of democracy was practiced, but did not apply to everyone. The population at the signing of the Constitution was four million, but only 200,000 Americans were eligible to vote.

African-Americans were not considered human beings and could be freely sold as merchandise. Women didn't have the right to hold public office or own real estate, much less cast a political vote.

No one spoke on behalf of the children, who were, as mentioned earlier, employed in the manual labor force at a young age. The protection of basic human rights existed only on paper. The poor were dependent on the generosity of whoever had a heart to help. The average family's goal was to have enough food to make it through to the next winter. Ample documentation illustrates the meager existence experienced by a bulk of the population.

This was not only the case in the United States, but in Europe as well. Life was hard, work was long, and pay was low. So much for the "good ol' days."

Capitalism ruled in those days; therefore, we may classify this as "historic capitalism." However, today's world has changed dramatically. We can justifiably claim that "social capitalism" is more applicable to our times.

The average worker wants a larger piece of the pie, and he is getting more and more of it. Not only can the average worker attain his "American dream" by owning a house, two cars, a boat and a swimming pool, but he can also afford to take a vacation once or twice a year. Two hundred years ago, the average family wouldn't even dream of taking a trip overseas. An entire year's income would be needed to cover the cost of a trip to Europe. But today, a round-trip ticket on an organized tour can be obtained for as low as two week's wages.

THE CAPITALIST CHANGEOVER

What happened during the last 200 years? Tax! The tax on earnings has completely changed the social fabric of this nation and the world.

The handicapped, who were previously considered societal "rejects" with no chance of making a living for themselves, were forced to depend on handouts. Today, Social Security and welfare assist the handicapped wherever possible.

In our western democratic world, no one is left out on the street to die. Innumerable government, private agencies and organizations ensure that all citizens have their basic needs met. Although it may be argued that much still needs to be done, we must admit that great progress has been seen, particularly within the last eighty years.

I want to stress the fact that my intention is not to endorse or oppose social services, but to factually analyze world development in order to show that all—capitalist, communist and socialist—must become one.

OWNING PRIVATE PROPERTY?

In a traditional sense, capitalism, communism, and socialism may have died, but all three are alive and well and exist in our modern society. This may sound contradictory, but it can be explained.

Capitalism no longer exists because capital, as it previously existed, does not. How come? Let me give you an example: Several years ago my son Micah came into my office and casually asked, "Have you paid the lease on your house?" I answered, "I don't lease my house, I bought it, it's mine." He answered, "Papa, I think you are mistaken, just try not paying your lease and the government will take away your property and lease it to someone else." What was he saying? Simply that private property has become subject to taxation; subsequently, socialism and communism are being re-introduced.

Who is the government? We the people! If I don't pay the taxes on my house, the government, ("We the people") will take away my private property, auction it to the highest bidder, and hopefully obtain taxes (lease) from the new owner.

SOCIAL AGRICULTURE

Agriculture is no longer the capital-based industry it used to be. Often farmers are paid not to plant a crop. Sometimes they receive large sums of subsidy to plant certain crops such as tobacco. The cattle industry is heavily subsidized through the leasing of government land for only pennies an acre. The government ("We the people") regulates the farmer's capital to insure that he will continue to produce food. Does this system work? Absolutely!

Agricultural systems are not only subsidized in the United States, but all over most of the world. As a result, the market is stocked with high quality, low priced food. Practically every nation tries to sell food to other countries. Is this a capitalistic system? Is it communist? Is it socialist? No. It is a mixture of the three.

HIGH-TECH SOCIALISM

Even high-tech industries such as IBM, General Electric and Boeing receive billions of dollars in subsidies. Who pays them? "We the people."

When the U.S. government cut subsidies for a planned passenger super jet to compete with the French-British Concorde, the entire project ended up in the "dead" file.

I believe this information shows that even the United States of America, considered to be the leading capitalist country in the world, is deeply entrenched in, and effectively implementing, social-capital distribution. Does it work? The answer is definitely "yes" because today, more people can share in the wealth of the nation.

HEALTHCARE SOCIALISM

A political battle regarding healthcare has been raging in the United States. Let's look at this matter objectively.

Does the United States practice capitalism, communism, or socialism? Most Americans would answer "capitalism." What are the facts? Sixty-five percent of Americans pay for healthcare insurance which is usually subsidized by their employers. But what about the 35 percent of Americans who do not have insurance? Who pays for them? The answer is very simple: The people who have health insurance pay for the ones who don't. This practice is known as communism.

I bring this matter to our attention so that we will understand that the world is changing and that all avenues lead toward world unity.

What will happen in the future? Depending on the country's level of wealth, more funds will be allocated to the poor while a larger majority of the population will be integrated into the economy, enjoying the prosperity of the nation.

Again, I must reiterate that this analysis is not based on my personal preference, but on existing factors as we watch the world develop into a super-state which will ultimately come under the leadership of the Antichrist.

In summary, the three political economic philosophies—capitalism, communism and socialism—are combining to create a new social/capital democracy.

You may wonder why I am presenting all of these facts when they don't seem to relate to the Bible. But in reality they do. Political, economic global unity is essential in fulfilling Bible prophecy. The Bible gives us history while it also outlines the present and future. When we attempt to deal with the future, we must first understand the past and present.

YOUR DESTINY

The world in which we live is only a temporary home for believers; we are just passing through. It makes no difference what nationality we are, under which government we live, or how rich, poor, simple or educated we are. Our ultimate goal as believers is the Lord Jesus Christ. The most important thing for a Christian to understand is that we have been bought by the blood of the Lamb, redeemed for eternity and chosen before the foundation of the world. When we understand our position, we learn to overlook or even disregard our condition because our position is settled once and for all in Jesus Christ. We have eternal life received by grace, *"...not of works, lest any man should boast."* Our condition may be quite different as we experience sickness, disappointment, tragedy and persecution, but in whatever circumstances we are found, our eternal position remains unchanged. The apostle Paul exclaimed with joy *"...I have learned, in whatsoever state I am, therewith to be content"* (Philippians 4:11).

Chapter 4

BABEL, BABYLON AND MYSTERY BABYLON

We have discussed the Trinity of God and elaborated on various other trinities such as man, the human race, politics, and the economy. Now let us look at the Babylon trinity:

1. The city of Babel and the tower the people aspired to build demonstrate humanity's desire to oppose God's law and unite for the sake of power and prestige.

2. The kingdom of Babylon accepted the separation of the nations with its different languages, traditions and cultures, but aimed to institute a one-world religion.

3. Mystery Babylon, the last Gentile superpower, unites the world politically, economically and religiously. The key to her success is "unity through diversity."

This is obviously a clever imitation of the father of lies, who knows that the Church is completely and perfectly united in the Lord, yet diverse while on earth. The Church is found in every country of the world. Its members speak different languages and practice varied traditions and cultures; however, the Church remains one.

Satan knew it would be impossible to make all people equal. He knew that only by means of diversity could the world be united. With these facts in mind, let us now look at the three important cornerstones in the development of the world's civilization.

BABEL

Following the catastrophic flood that destroyed every living person with the exception of Noah and his family, we find a listing of his descendants; Shem, Ham and Japheth, recorded in Genesis 10. God's original intention to fill the earth was given to Adam and Eve, now it would be fulfilled by Noah's descendants.

As previously mentioned, there is ample reason to believe that at one time the earth consisted of only one continent. Although there is no definite proof of this theory, Genesis 10:32 concludes with the words, *"These are the families of the sons of Noah, after their generations, in their nations: and by these were the nations divided in the earth after the flood."*

Chapter 11 illustrates opposition to God's intention, *"...the whole earth was of one language, and of one speech"* (Genesis 11:1). The short story recorded in Genesis 11 summarizes man's opposition to God.

Reading verses 3 and 4 we notice the words "us" and "we" are repeated several times, *"And they said one to another, Go to, let us make brick, and burn them throughly. And they had brick for stone, and slime had they for mortar. And they said, Go to, let us build us a city and a tower, whose top may reach unto heaven; and let us make us a name, lest we be scattered abroad upon the face of the whole earth."* Since there is no mention of a leader or king, we must conclude that this was the institution of the first "we the people" democracy.

What was their intention? They wanted to build a city, which in and of itself is harmless.

I don't believe there was anything wrong with building the city, nor do I think God would have opposed it. However, the Bible reveals something else, *"...and a tower whose top may reach unto heaven."* Reading this statement we realize that not only was the people's intention to "live and let live," but they also wanted to form their own religion through which they could reach heaven.

The next few words *"...let us make us a name"* reveal the fact that fame and fortune were also involved. And then we read, *"...lest we be scattered abroad upon the face of the whole earth...."* Wasn't that exactly the opposite of what God told them to do? Didn't He say to replenish the earth? This was blatant rebellion against the Living God!

Therefore, Babel can be summarized as man's attempt to glorify himself and his works, subsequently establishing his own religion in order to reach heaven. The act exemplifies the age-old religious philosophy of working to attain salvation. This "Babel" religion is still practiced today. It is a religion of works which teaches, if you do such and such you will please God and enter heaven.

TOWER OF BABEL IN EUROPE?

Quite often I read about man's vain attempt to rebuild the Tower of Babel using the European Union as an example. However, based on prevailing facts and European laws, such is not the case. In fact, just the opposite is true; they are determined to keep the diversity of languages. At this time, the 15-member states speak 11 languages. During all European parliamentary functions, ten languages are simultaneously translated. Preparations have been made for an additional 12 languages, if and when eastern European states are accepted into the Union. Therefore, Europe is not resurrecting the Tower of Babel.

The Tower of Babel society was built on the new continents. For example, immigrants who came from dozens of countries, speaking multiple languages, were forced to speak either English or French in Canada, English in the United States, Spanish in Mexico, and Portuguese in Brazil. In North America, where practically every nation is represented, one language was a key to success. You will not get very far in the United States if you don't speak English.

Every time I read this story, it strikes me as odd that God is the originator of diverse languages and opposes a unified language. Surely if we all spoke one language there would have been less conflicts and controversy and perhaps fewer wars. Apparently that is not the case. While language diversity has certainly contributed to war, it hasn't been the biggest factor.

Major wars have been avoided since World War II, not because of language but because of economics. Our global world is so interrelated that any major war would cause the collapse of the entire global infrastructure resulting in unprecedented catastrophe.

THE KINGDOM OF BABYLON

The difference between Babel and Babylon lies in the fact that Babel was a functioning democracy ruled by the people. However, Babylon was ruled by royal monarchy; the king was the authority and at his word, all of the Babylonian elite would have lost their lives, were it not for one Jewish servant named Daniel.

King Nebuchadnezzar had a dream and when he awoke he had forgotten what he dreamed. As was customary, he called his advisors much like in the United States, the President would call his cabinet for advice as to what course of action he should take.

King Nebuchadnezzar told his advisors, *"...the astrologers, the sorcerers, and the Chaldeans..."* that he had a dream that disturbed him very much and wanted to know what it meant. Those poor fellows were expected to tell him the meaning of the dream without even being told what the dream was about: *"The Chaldeans answered before the king, and said, There is not a man upon the earth that can shew the king's matter: therefore there is no king, lord, nor ruler, that asked such things at any magician, or astrologer, or Chaldean. And it is a rare thing that the king requireth, and there is none other that can shew it before the king, except the gods, whose dwelling is not with flesh"* (Daniel 2:10–11).

Just recently when we read this part of Daniel in our

family devotions, my oldest son Joel remarked, "You've got to give these people credit, they were honest. Although they were pagans, they had the decency to say they didn't know. If King Nebuchadnezzar presented his case to today's intellectuals and advisors in Washington, he would have been given a volume of answers based on the imagination of the individuals." How true that is. Even our beloved former President Ronald Reagan apparently relied on advice he received from his wife Nancy that originated with the occult. So, in that respect, we must give credit to Nebuchadnezzar and his Babylonian system.

When Daniel interprets the dream, which described a great image composed of gold, silver, brass, iron and clay, we read the following in verses 37 and 38: *"Thou, O king, art a king of kings: for the God of heaven hath given thee a kingdom, power, and strength, and glory...Thou art this head of gold."* Of course gold is more precious than silver, brass, iron, or clay. Nebuchadnezzar is identified by God as the best form of government of all the Gentile powers.

After Daniel revealed the meaning of his dream, the king confessed, *"...Of a truth it is, that your God is a God of gods, and a Lord of kings, and a revealer of secrets..."* (Daniel 2:47).

THE IMAGE OF GOLD

Unfortunately Nebuchadnezzar's conversion was purely emotional. In the next chapter he constructed *"...an image of gold, whose height was threescore cubits, and the breadth thereof six cubits..."* (Daniel 3:1). Why? To create a unified form of worship.

Its apparent that Nebuchadnezzar did not outlaw all other religions or forbid the worship of other gods. But he specifically desired that his image should be the center of worship: *"...To you it is commanded, O people, nations, and languages, That at what time ye hear the sound of the cornet, flute, harp, sackbut, psaltery, dulcimer, and all kinds of musik, ye fall down and worship the golden image that Nebuchadnezzar the king hath set up"* (Daniel 3:4–5). There was only one requirement expected from the people; they were to *"...fall down and worship the golden image."*

In today's language, that means you can continue to be a Christian, Buddhist, Muslim, Hindu, or Catholic and pledge your loyalty, "One nation under God;" just don't name your god. You don't have to deny your heritage, tradition, or religion; you can worship this image but just be sure not to offend anybody else by naming your god!

That should remind us of the Ecumenical Movement working through the World Council of Churches. It suggests we follow its liberally-defined guidelines without rejecting, offending, or insulting any other religious beliefs.

IMAGE OF A GOD

I run the risk of being chided by fellow believers, but such is the case with phrases such as, "in God we trust" or "one nation under God." These phrases are not specific; therefore, anyone can say them. Anyone can recite the Pledge of Allegiance regardless of what god they believe in. An overwhelming majority of the population believes in God, however, it is the name of Jesus that is always conveniently omitted. I have yet to find Jesus' name mentioned in any official document such as the Declaration of Independence or the Constitution of any country. Why? First, it might offend others, and second, the Bible does not endorse a political identity in the name Jesus Christ. The Bible teaches that no nation on the face of the earth will become an entity under the Lord Jesus Christ.

THE NUMBER SIX

Daniel 3 also reveals the sinister number six. The erected image was *"...threescore cubits in height"* which equals sixty, and the *"...breadth thereof six cubits."*

The six musical instruments used to announce the worship are listed three times in verse 10, they are: 1) *"...the cornet,* 2) *flute,* 3) *harp,* 4) *sackbut,* 5) *psaltery,* and 6) *dulcimer..."* (Daniel 3:10).

GLOBAL MUSIC

It makes no difference how you view today's modern rock-and-roll music, because it has now become globally accepted. I have spoken to many Christians who defend the use of evangelical rock-and-roll as a tool to call lost souls to Christ. There is no doubt in my mind that many have come to believe in Jesus during such concerts. But it is significant to note that for the first time since Nebuchadnezzar's rule, no other music but rock-and-roll has become as recognized worldwide.

During a recent visit to Germany, the capital of classical

music, I was quite surprised when looking for traditional German folk music in a discount store. Over ninety percent of its shelves were stocked with rock music. My wife and I then found a small corner marked "Deutsche Musick." That does not mean that rock-and-roll music is more demonic than traditional "Deutsche Musick" or classical music, for that matter. However, it does seem rather strange that for the first time in history, we have a type of international music under which all nations can unify.

I must admit that judging between various types of music is not my area of expertise, although I have read a number of articles in which authors have convincingly shown that rock-and-roll music is satanically inspired. The issue is not who is right or wrong, but simply that this music does exist and is globally accepted by virtually all people. Thus, for the first time in history, we have a global, unifying music under which all people can identify, and that is an extremely significant point.

GLOBAL POLITICS

There are many different systems of democracy, but no one can deny that this political philosophy primarily identified as "We the people" is now ruling the world. Woe unto any country that opposes this system.

Just a quick glance at some of the nations outside of the "democratic world family" such as Cuba, North Vietnam, and Libya prove that they are experiencing significant setbacks because of their refusal to comply.

JEWS REFUSE THE IMAGE

Nebuchadnezzar was not successful in religiously uniting the people. Three young Jews defeated him by placing their faith and trust in the God of Israel. It is ironic that Nebuchadnezzar, who caused the image to be erected with the goal of unifying religion, was the one who later said, *"...I make a decree, That every people, nation, and language, which speak any thing amiss against the God of Shadrach, Meshach, and Abednego, shall be cut in pieces, and their houses shall be made a dunghill: because there is no other God that can deliver after this sort"* (Daniel 3:29). God works in mysterious ways. In this case, the pagan king became the greatest evangelist of that time!

MYSTERY BABYLON

"And upon her forehead was a name written, MYSTERY, BABYLON THE GREAT, THE MOTHER OF HARLOTS AND ABOMINATIONS OF THE EARTH" (Revelation 17:5).

People are fascinated by the word "mystery," which indicates something that cannot fully be explained. That is one of the reasons why mystery movies and books are so popular. A mystery allows the author to liberally use his or her imagination. It doesn't have to be explained if its a mystery. All theories can be entertained because that is the essence of "mystery."

The Bible is the Word of God given to man in order to understand God's counsel. Why does the Bible say, "Mystery Babylon" and not "Mystery Jerusalem" or "Mystery Rome?" We know both Jerusalem and Rome play a central role in endtime developments. So why

Mystery Babylon? Does this city even exist? If it's the ancient Babylon located on the Euphrates River, then it does not; all that remains is ruins. Some of the walls and buildings have been rebuilt as tourist attractions under the leadership of Saddam Hussein, but that's about it. Babylon does not exist! The words prophesied by Jeremiah the prophet had come to pass, *"And Babylon shall become heaps, a dwellingplace for dragons, an astonishment, and an hissing, without an inhabitant"* (Jeremiah 51:37).

REVEALING MYSTERY BABYLON

During the past decades, rumors were spread and books written about the possibility of ancient Babylon being fully rebuilt as a functioning city, ultimately becoming the capital city of the world. There are several flaws in this theory:

1. Revelation 17:6: *"...I saw the woman drunken with the blood of the saints, and with the blood of the martyrs of Jesus...."* This simple statement knocks ancient Babylon out of contention for the title "Mystery Babylon."

2. In verse 9 is a geographic reference that does not apply to ancient Babylon: *"The seven heads are seven mountains, on which the woman sitteth."* The woman the Bible is speaking of here is the one we read about in the beginning: *"MYSTERY BABYLON, THE GREAT, THE MOTHER OF HARLOTS AND ABOMINATIONS OF THE EARTH."* This woman sits on seven mountains, which is a topographical reference. To be sure that the woman represents a city, verse 18 says, *"And the woman which thou sawest is that great city, which reigneth over the kings of the*

earth." Ancient Babylon is not built on mountains, but is located on flat land on the banks of the Euphrates River.

3. Furthermore, we have a political, economic, and religious reference that says, *"For all nations have drunk of the wine of the wrath of her fornication, and the kings of the earth have committed fornication with her, and the merchants of the earth are waxed rich through the abundance of her delicacies"* (Revelation 18:3). This verse causes us to question whether there is any such city in the world to which presidents, prime ministers and government leaders travel? The answer is "yes": the Vatican in Rome.

These three points should clearly show that Mystery Babylon cannot physically be located where ancient Babylon once stood.

FORNICATION SUCCESS

Fornication is defined as an illegal and immoral sexual act; therefore, by interpretation, the mixing of politics and religion can also constitute fornication.

Economically speaking, the Western world is becoming richer and more prosperous than ever. It is built on the principles of Roman democracy and free trade, including the freedom of religion. Although it is not true capitalism, this system is currently marching victoriously across the globe. Where does it all come from? Rome.

THE GROWING EUROPE

At the time of this writing, the European Union, which is an outgrowth of the Treaties of Rome, signed by six-member nations in 1957, has become the greatest economic colossus the world has ever seen. But this is only the beginning. Over a dozen nations are standing in line with application in hand, hoping for acceptance into the European Union.

By way of explanation, we must add that the European Union does not exclusively constitute the world's last power structure. *"All nations"* will participate in *"...the abundance of her delicacies"*; therefore, Mystery Babylon must be worldwide.

ONE RELIGION...MANY GODS

The *Columbia Viking Desk Encyclopedia* documents the following under Babylonian religions:

> The religion of the whole Tigris-Euphrates valley was really one, with many local gods. Dominant gods were determined by dominant cities (e.g. when Babylon was paramount, Marduk, or Bel or Baal, was king of gods). Priests were very powerful. The rich mythology of Babylon, further elaborated by Assyria, was preserved in cuneiform writing on clay tablets. It included stories of [the] creation of [the] world, of a flood covering the whole world, journey of Ishtar to underworld, and legends of gods and heroes. Babylon was indebted to Sumerian culture for its religion, and its great towers (suggesting BABEL) were reminiscent of Sumerian worship of high places.

Fascinating! One religion with many gods. That is precisely what's in the works today. The nations strive to be a pluralistic society, tolerant and acceptant of each other's religions, cultures, languages and political philosophies under the auspices of democracy, free trade, and religious plurality. When viewing Mystery Babylon's description from this angle, we begin to understand why it is called Mystery Babylon. While the center of activity is clearly identified in the Bible and cannot be any other city but Rome, the effects are far-reaching and global.

Let's reassure ourselves that globalism is the foreseeable trend of the future, not based on opinion, but on the Word of God.

In Daniel 2:35, it was prophesied that all Gentile political identities would be destroyed, *"...that no place was found for them: and the stone that smote the image became a great mountain, and filled the whole earth."*

Verse 39 says that the next two kingdoms, *"...shall bear rule over all the earth."*

In Daniel 7:23 we read, *"Thus he said, The fourth beast shall be the fourth kingdom upon earth, which shall be diverse from all kingdoms, and shall devour the whole earth, and shall tread it down, and break it in pieces."*

Daniel 7:23 is in perfect harmony with Revelation 13:3 which says, *"...and all the world wondered after the beast."*

The Antichrist is the epitome of the rulers described in verse 8, *"And all that dwell upon the earth shall worship him...."*

FINAL WARNING

Believers who obey the prophetic Word will notice that we are living in the last stages of the endtimes. However, an increasing number of unbelievers are also expressing a growing concern that a global world is already in the making. Some are beginning to realize the danger of a possible one-person rule, which could lead to the greatest dictatorship the world has ever seen.

But the leaders of the world are working feverishly to unify the planet. It is assumed that when we are all united, wars will cease, prosperity will become a global reality, crime will be eliminated, poverty done away with, and the result will be a peaceful world society living in harmony with nature.

However, this theory clearly contradicts the Holy Scriptures which say that the moment man believes he has reached the stage of global peace and prosperity, the most horrendous days the world has ever experienced will begin. First Thessalonians 5:3 says, *"For when they shall say, Peace and safety; then sudden destruction cometh upon them, as travail upon a woman with child; and they shall not escape."*

There is only one escape from the judgment to come. It is not an escape to a new philosophy, or a different type of government, but is directed toward the One who said, *"I am the door: by me if any man enter in, he shall be saved..."* (John 10:9). How can you enter? By faith. Believe that Jesus, the Son of God, has paid for your sins with His own blood on Calvary's cross. John 3:36 guarantees, *"He that believeth on the Son hath everlasting life: and he that believeth not the Son shall not see life; but the wrath of God abideth on him."*

Chapter 5

THE ART OF DECEPTION

God gave the Ten Commandments to the Israelites through His servant Moses. These commands were designed to remind Israel that there is only one God and He alone is worthy of worship. God's first commandment to Israel is extremely important. It does not say that you should not have other gods, but you should have no other gods *"...before me."* The Jewish Tenakh, which is translated from the Hebrew says, *"You shall have no other gods besides me."* In other words, "If you want to serve other gods, go ahead, it's your decision—but you can't serve Me at the same time!" Later on in history, Elijah the prophet challenged a backslidden Israel: *"...if the Lord be God, follow Him, but if Baal, follow him."* It was either one or the other.

When analyzing other religions, it is important to remember this fundamental truth. The basic principles of the Ten Commandments are respected around the globe. Although they were addressed to Israel, the nations of the world—despite a diversity in culture and varying degrees of civilization—are all in virtual agreement with these tenets. I have tried to find a nation where stealing is encouraged, killing is rewarded and where it was legal to tell lies, but have found no such place. Depending on the type of government, violation against such and other laws are punished according to the law of the land. However, no country rewards the above-mentioned crimes.

The Ten Commandments were designed to teach respect for God, family and property. This was, and remains, the law for Israel: *"Thou shalt not covet thy neighbour's house, thou shalt not covet thy neighbour's wife, nor his manservant, nor his maidservant, nor his ox, nor his ass, nor any thing that is thy neighbour's"* (Exodus 20:17).

TEN COMMANDMENTS IN SCHOOL

I am aware that many will disagree with the statement I am about to make, but based on my understanding of the Scripture, and the simple fact that the Law was given to Israel and not the nations, I see no reason for Christians to fight to have the Ten Commandments publicly displayed.

The assumption that posting the Ten Commandments will have some kind of magical effect on a nation's citizens is equivalent to idolatry. The bottom line is this: In their fullness, the Ten Commandments cannot be kept by anyone. Some brethren teach that the fourth commandment is the most important; therefore, the Jewish sabbath should be kept by all believers. Usually when debating this subject, those who refuse to heed the fourth commandment are accused of picking and choosing which commandments are suitable to follow. Later on in this chapter, we will see that anyone who tries to keep the Ten Commandments will soon realize that it simply cannot be done. If we were humanly capable of keeping the commandments, we would have no need for a Savior. For a religious ordinance such as Churchianity or Freemasonry, which thrive on this type of religiosity, keeping the Ten Commandments may be very impressive. But for the Church, God has not commanded the Gentiles to be concerned with the Law, except of course, those of criminal nature which are kept by the nations as I have already mentioned.

THOU SHALT NOT COVET

The tenth commandment in particular stands in total contradiction to today's modern, democratic, social/capitalistic system. This commandment does not concern itself with stealing, which is already covered in the eighth commandment; rather, the tenth commandment specifically speaks of coveting or desiring something that does not belong to us. This concept goes against all modern business practices around the world. I seriously doubt that any of today's global companies would call an executive board meeting aimed at discouraging success or competition among their executives.

For example, consider General Motors and Ford Motor Company. During a periodic review of progress, the Chairman of the Board might take the podium and say, "Ladies and Gentlemen, it has come to our attention that Ford Motor Company has achieved a 35% profit margin and their shares have increased in value by 22%. As long as I am Chairman of the Board, I would rather you not desire their success, but be satisfied with our 12% profit margin and 2% raise in stocks." In such a case, that Chairman of the Board would barely have time to finish his announcement before he was fired. Our social-capitalism actually thrives on competition; each wants what the other has, and if possible, more.

ISRAEL TO BE SEGREGATED

Why then did God give the tenth commandment to the Israelites? God's desire for His people is for them to be separate from the nations of the world as revealed in His Word, *"For thou art an holy people unto the LORD thy God, and the LORD hath chosen thee to be a peculiar people unto himself, above all the nations that are upon the earth"* (Deuteronomy 14:2). Therefore, in its entirety, the tenth commandment cannot apply to the nations. The global economic system would collapse overnight if we followed the law to the letter. The Great Depression of 1929 would be remembered as simply a minor inconvenience if compared with the unspeakable catastrophe that would follow if the tenth commandment were implemented as global law.

A number of the laws God gave were designed to regulate property among the Israelites. For example, land was not to be sold, *"The land shall not be sold for ever: for the land is mine; for ye are strangers and sojourners with me"* (Leviticus 25:23). This perpetual deed to land in Israel is another important law that cannot be practiced among the nations.

Biblical laws are designed for the biblical land and its

biblical people for a very specific purpose. If a Jew experienced financial ruin, he would temporarily lose his possessions; however, God made a provision, *"And if thy brother that dwelleth by thee be waxen poor, and be sold unto thee; thou shalt not compel him to serve as a bondservant: But as an hired servant, and as a sojourner, he shall be with thee, and shall serve thee unto the year of jubile: And then shall he depart from thee, both he and his children with him, and shall return unto his own family, and unto the possession of his fathers shall he return"* (Leviticus 25:39–41). Think of what would happen if all long-term loans, bonds and mortgages were voided in the fiftieth year: the world economic system would collapse.

God repeatedly makes it clear that Israel is His servant. The last verse of chapter 25 says, *"For unto me the children of Israel are servants; they are my servants whom I brought forth out of the land of Egypt: I am the LORD your God"* (verse 55). Quite simply, this doesn't apply to the nations of the world.

BLESSING OR SUCCESS?

The words "blessing" and "success" are of equal importance to most people. The word "blessing" is primarily based on the passages of Scripture where we read that God blessed those who were obedient to His Word. Christians desire blessings from the Lord. Blessing is more important than success, and success has no direct relation to blessing. One may be extremely successful without the Lord's blessing, but that type of success is only temporary. To be blessed by the Lord does not always mean that a person is successful. The heroes of faith listed in Hebrews 11 were anything but successful; however, they were blessed servants of the Lord, *"And others had trial of cruel mockings and scourgings, yea, moreover of bonds and imprisonment: They were stoned, they were sawn asunder, were tempted, were slain with the sword: they wandered about in sheepskins and goatskins; being destitute, afflicted tormented; (Of whom the world was not worthy:) they wandered in deserts, and in mountains, and in dens and caves of the earth"* (Hebrews 11:36–38).

In our modern world, we notice that the ungodly relish in great success. Statistics show that on the average, sodomites are more successful than others. Additionally, no one can deny the success of Freemason lodge members. The success of people who do not believe in the God of creation through the name of Jesus is very evident.

On a national and financial level, Japan is one of the richest countries in the world. Based on information I have found in the *CIA 1998 Fact Book,* Japan is not listed as having any external debt. Compare that with the United States, who was listed with a debt of $862 billion for 1995. United States economic aid to other countries was listed at 9.721 billion for 1993, compared with the tiny island of Japan—whose labor force is less than half that of the United States—who contributed 8.3 billion in foreign aid. I believe we can say with reasonable assurance that Japan's riches are based on success. We must keep in mind that they are a Buddhist nation; therefore, blessings from the God of Israel, whom they outrightly reject, is not applicable. We can use this same rule of measure with the rest of the world's nations.

ISRAEL'S SUCCESS BASED ON BLESSING

When we talk about blessing and success we must look at Israel, a nation different from all others. What does the Bible says about these people? *"And the LORD shall make thee plenteous in goods, in the fruit of thy body, and in the fruit of thy cattle, and in the fruit of thy ground, in the land which the LORD sware unto thy fathers to give thee. The LORD shall open unto thee his good treasure, the heaven to give the rain unto thy land in his season, and to bless all the work of thine hand: and thou shalt lend unto many nations, and thou shalt not borrow. And the LORD shall make thee the head, and not the tail; and thou shalt be above only, and thou shalt not be beneath; if that thou hearken unto the commandments of the LORD thy God, which I command thee this day, to observe and to do them"* (Deuteronomy 28:11–13). That is an example of God blessing Israel above all the nations on the face of the earth both materially and financially.

But notice that this blessing comes with a condition: *"... if that thou hearken unto the commandments of the LORD to observe and to do them."* Bible readers know about the conditions set forth by God for the recipient of such blessings. We also know that Israel's economy was based on a theocratic system that did not allow the rich to take advantage of the poor for an indefinite amount of time. All debt was considered obsolete after 49 years of servitude and was followed by a new economic system the following year.

This type of system no longer exists. We live in a world that practices Roman democracy and is based on Roman laws; therefore, we are not national candidates for the blessings described in the Bible.

NATIONAL BLESSING?

Second Chronicles 7:14 is an often-quoted verse that is only applicable to Israel: *"If my people, which are called by my name, shall humble themselves, and pray, and seek my face, and turn from their wicked ways; then will I hear from heaven, and will forgive their sin, and will heal their land."* Why can't this blessing be applied to our nation? Because there is no such thing as a Christian nation. Unless a person has placed faith in Jesus Christ, and is born again of His Spirit, he is not considered one of the Lord's people. We do not constitute the nation, but are a minority among the nations.

The promise of 2nd Chronicles 7:14 belongs in the realm of blessings, not success, and is exclusively meant for Israel, but spiritually directed to the Church.

ANTICHRIST MUST BE SUCCESSFUL

These few words of explanation should show that in order for the Antichrist to deceive the world he must create a successful economic, political, military and religious system that would look very much like the one promised to Israel in the Bible.

In Isaiah 54:17 we read the following in regard to Israel, *"No weapon that is formed against thee shall prosper...."* The imitation is found in Revelation 13:4, *"...Who is like unto the beast? who is able to make war with him?"* Apparently he will have superior military power so that no nation will be able to oppose him in war.

But absolute victory is only promised to the children of Israel and has always been based on the condition that they follow the Word of God.

SELF-EXALTATION

Daniel 11:36 describes the Antichrist with the following words, *"And the king shall do according to his will; and he shall exalt himself, and magnify himself above every god, and shall speak marvellous things against the God of gods, and shall prosper till the indignation be accomplished: for that that is determined shall be done."* This is extreme success. He has an excellent self-image in that he will "exalt" and "magnify" himself. He doesn't need any special sessions with a psychologist in order to build up his self-esteem; he is the epitome of self-esteem.

It's almost unbelievable how self-esteem and self-love are now being preached from pulpits in churches around the world. If you need further confirmation of this fact, just take a trip to your local Christian bookstore and you will find the shelves lined with titles of books that promote "self." No longer do we read that we are to take up our cross daily and follow Christ. Apparently this philosophy is old fashioned. What's "in" today is how to look better, feel better, improve your marriage, love forever, be a better husband, and have a successful family. Lately, a popular subject on the market addresses how Christians can get rich quick! I am fully aware that each of these and many other subjects I have not listed are written because of the author's motivation by a genuine concern for the well being of Christians, but we cannot deny the fact that the balance was tipped over long ago and is now directed toward self: What's in it for me? How can I benefit? Is there any value I can gather for myself?

HOW CAN I BENEFIT?

A recent article appeared in a trade publication that dealt exclusively with direct mail and hammered home the fact that if you don't offer people something from which they can benefit, you are basically wasting your time with the offer.

The Bible says that the Antichrist shall prosper. Prosperity is a result of success and is exactly what the world's economy and financial empires are built upon.

The entire world is now following in the footsteps of the exaltation of the Antichrist. This philosophy is nothing other than an imitation of the verse which states, *"Wherefore God also hath highly exalted him, and given him a name which is above every name"* (Philippians 2:9).

Notice the contrast: the Antichrist exalts himself, but Jesus is exalted by God. It's no wonder the devil tried so desperately to con Jesus into falling down and worshipping him during the temptation in the desert. He wanted to imitate Jesus because of Him it is written, *"...That at the name of Jesus every knee should bow, of things in heaven, and things in earth, and things under the earth; And that every tongue should confess that Jesus Christ is Lord, to the glory of God the Father"* (Philippians 2:10–11).

The Bible makes it clear that *every* knee will bow—not just a select group of people from certain countries. It is for this reason the false prophet will lead mankind into building an image of the beast and "...*the image of the beast should both speak, and cause that as many as would not worship the image of the beast should be killed*" (Revelation 13:15). We will discuss this subject at length when we target religious deception in another chapter.

THE ART OF BUSINESS DECEPTION

Relating to business practice and finances, I would like to quote from pages 6 and 8 of the February 2000 issue of *Eternal Value Review* by Wilfred J. Hahn:

Widespread Deception. No question. It's prophesied that deceit will be a hallmark of the kingdom of the last days. Right from the prophecies of Isaiah, Daniel and others, we are clearly instructed that the last regime—the one that ultimately gives rise to the final rebellion against God—is one marked by deceit. Among many scriptures attesting to this situation are these: "*[...] understanding dark sentences* (verse 23); *[...] he shall cause craft to prosper*" (verse 25); "*...by peace shall destroy many*" (verse 25); "*...he shall come in peaceably...shall work deceitfully...enter peaceably...speak lies at one table...*" (Daniel 11:21,23,24,27). Also, Apostle Paul talks about the "*mystery of iniquity already at work*" which refers to the inspiration and diabolic strategist behind the advance of the endtime regime. Scripture is clear on this point: deception is a key characteristic of endtime world systems—financial, religious, political or otherwise. Is that already true today?

With respect to present financial and economic systems, any financial analyst with a bit of common sense must agree that these are riddled with falsehoods. This topic alone is worthy of a book. I could probably think of a hundred or more statistical falsehoods, false doctrines, faulty economic theories—some of them probably demonically inspired—that play an accepted role. Without a doubt, today's global financial systems are perched upon an unstable tower of intrigue, confidence games, insider activity, conspiracies etc. These practices and values are not just those of rogues and mavericks, but rather are institutionalized at the highest levels. This overall condition is best reflected by this quote: "Heaven no longer provides a strong incentive to do good these days, especially to the pragmatists of the world, including hard-bitten corporate raiders, investment bankers, politicians, and business people."

The fractional reserve banking system, aided and abetted by central banks—a system that has now extended to almost every nation around the world—is only one example, although a key one. Its very essence is a confidence game, albeit one that has been perpetuated successfully for several centuries. Were every depositor ever to ask a bank to make good their promise to pay back their demand deposit all at the same time, this institution would collapse instantly. As such, the bank's promise is really a deception. Imagine if God's promises to us were dependent on a fractional reserve system? They'd only be available to a select few and not open to all. Like a theater fire, only the first through the door would be saved.

Deception is actually an honored business tactic these days as long as it doesn't take the form of an outright, brazen lie. Successful businesses are expected to shroud their strategies in secrecy. Public relations officers of major companies listed on stock exchanges choose their words extremely carefully so as to avoid any negative impact upon their stock price. What is not said is just as important as what is. Positive news travels quickly; negative announcements arrive on the back of a turtle or aren't mentioned at all. Public relations (PR) consultants—popularly called spin-doctors—are in high demand. As an article about public relations business opined, "it is a somewhat sleazy occupation, requiring few skills or qualifications other than a careless disdain for inconvenient truths and a voracious appetite for the free lunch." Yet, PR consultancy is a growth business.

The morality of many generally accepted business practices remains questionable. Yet, it is interesting that business ethics is an increasingly popular field of research. There are dozens of ethics centers in North America dedicated to its study. Many Fortune 500 businesses today employ managers of business ethics. What kind of business ethics is this? Whatever the case, it concerns itself with codes of conduct in a business world that is essentially deceptive.

Here is an interesting anomaly: Why are stock market analysts more likely to issue "buy" recommendations than "sells"? It used to be the norm that for every 10 "buy" reports, only one "sell" recommendation was made. That statistic displays extreme bias. However, in recent years, this dishonest tendency has become even more extreme. A 1999 survey of stock market analysts and public companies concludes that 90% of all analysts are afraid of the repercussions of issuing a sell recommendation. Therefore, it is not surprising that a recent snapshot of over 27,700 analyst reports recently found that less than 1% of these advised that investors should sell a stock. Such a skewed slanting of the facts really amounts to an exercise of deception. Only those opinions which placate greed and promote gains are emphasized and encouraged. Negative news or unfavorable opinions are suppressed or conveniently ignored.

Accountants, too, are under ever greater pressure to falsify figures. Invariably, these misstatements almost always serve to raise reported profits. A National Association of Accountants study of managers reported that 87% of them are willing to commit some type of accounting fraud.

While I have only commented upon North American trends so far, my observation is that these trends are worse elsewhere. Though there are abuses, North America still ranks as one of the best places for disclosure when gauged on a world scale. In Asia, for example, it is extremely rare that anyone might publicly announce something that might be seen to be even vaguely negative for the cause of prosperity. The public relations practices in Continental Europe leave much to be desired as well.

Lastly, there's not much hope that the deceptive conditions of our times will improve if the attitudes of recent graduating classes are any indication. Survey after survey shows that there's an admitted carelessness with the truth. Disturbingly, business students are most prone to practice deceit. A survey of MBA students at Tulane University revealed that no less than 76% of them were willing to fudge company profit figures. Another survey of business students from 31 universities revealed that 95% cheated during high school and college.

No doubt, deception runs rampant in the world of finance and commerce. It's the accepted norm. It's the grease of prosperity in this day and age.

This article was written by a man who makes his living in the financial world. In his editor's note in the same publication he says among other things:

In my experience, not one of the godly characteristics cited above is held in any regard today in the corporate workplace. There are exceptions, of course. But the general reality is that values such as these get in the way of making money. Practice them and you will soon be targeted as a misfit. The notion that you will be rewarded materially by living a godly life in the corporate marketplace is fast becoming a delusion.

Lies and deception are not the exception, they are the norm!

THE ART OF POLITICAL DECEPTION

When Daniel received his vision of endtime events, he spoke of a military conflict in which the Antichrist would have with the *"...king of the south"* and then wrote, *"And both these kings' hearts shall be to do mischief, and they shall speak lies at one table; but it shall not prosper: for yet the end shall be at the time appointed"* (Daniel 11:27). Martin Luther translated this verse with the words, *"Both of the kings will think in their heart how to cause damage to the other...."* The Jewish Tanakh reads, *"The minds of both kings will be bent on evil...while sitting at the table together, they will lie to each other...."*

Most of us may not be fully aware of the fact that this is standard procedure. Today's diplomats are schooled in the language of lies. Words are twisted beyond recognition and intentions are so veiled that specially-trained interpreters are needed to identify the original motive of the statement.

When a political leader makes an important statement while addressing the nation, news editors follow the presentation and analyze what was "really" said.

We all know that's part of democracy, and democracy is globally proclaimed as a political philosophy that guarantees freedom to all people. In our present day, we cannot argue with the success of the democratic system. After all, who would want to live under communism or a dictatorship? Surely no one who has lived under democracy would choose any other system. But the great British statesman, Winston Churchill, once said, "Democracy is the worst form of government but it is the best we have."

We enjoy the freedom of casting our vote for certain candidates. We would argue that our system gives us a chance to get rid of politicians who oppose public opinion. Above all, we can rightly brag that democracy is definitely a success in our day. This is particularly true since the fall of the Iron Curtain and the bankruptcy of the communist Soviet Union.

But such statements overlook the fact that in the long run, the entire system is designed against God and His anointed.

Just recently my wife Ruth called my attention to an article published in the German edition of *Focus* newsweekly stating that former East Germans have become casualties from heart attacks at an increase of 50% over the last decade. This was very significant to those who grew up in a democratic world; we feel at home and at ease with its rules and regulations. However, former communists were suddenly faced with bankruptcy and forced to enter the open door of democratic capitalism. They have experienced the evolutionary process of capital democracy in just a few years. Most of us in the West know of no other government but democracy. But these former communists experienced a shock of which many lead to a heart attack.

HOT WATER AND THE FROG

During one of our prophecy conferences, a speaker offered a vivid example of evolutionary deception: "Scientists have tested the reaction of a frog placed in hot water. When placed in hot water, the frog jumps out. But when placed in colder water, where slowly, the temperature was increased until boiling, the frog stays in the water until he dies."

Therefore, the assumption that we will not be deceived, that our system is fool-proof and that our Constitution is our ultimate security, is indeed wishful thinking.

Economic deception is running just as rampant today as political deception. It has become the accepted norm in our extremely successful society. We are as used to it as the frog was in the increasingly hot water.

SELF-DECEPTION

Salespeople today are trained to build an illusionary castle so that potential clients cannot refuse to buy the product.

In the late 60's, my wife and I went to Florida for a week of vacation. We were invited to attend a land development seminar. As a special bonus we were promised dinner with all the trimmings and a free gift. After enjoying a sensational meal, we were led into an elaborately-decorated office where we were required to attend a one-hour presentation for this planned development. All the advantages were listed in such a way that buying land now would result in a fantastic investment guaranteeing multiple returns. We were informed that about 80% of their potential clients jumped at the opportunity to purchase this land. Of course, we belonged to the 20% who politely thanked the salesman for his time, the interesting presentation and the wonderful meal, and then left. But I have to admit that saying "no" to such an offer was probably received as insulting to the salesman because he made it look as though he was giving us our once-in-a-lifetime opportunity to become rich. He made it seem like he had reserved this lot especially for us and had done everything in his power to enable us to become the owners of this valuable piece of real estate. Wow!

SUPERMARKET DECEPTION

Even supermarkets use deceptive advertising to lure customers into their stores to buy their products while they enrich themselves with the customers' finances. Whoever tells the best lie and remains within the legal parameters of the written law is the winner.

Occasionally we notice an advertisement in our daily newspaper from a grocery chain we will refer to as "A." This store is attempting to show that its prices are lower than grocery chain "B." "A" goes shopping at "B." After accumulating approximately 50 items which are sold at a higher price than their "A" store, they stop. Now they go shopping at their own store "A." Obviously, all the identical items are cheaper at store "A" because they were pre-selected. Now "A" will show the original receipts from store "A" and store "B." The reader can compare and clearly see that store "A" is cheaper than store "B." But what is being hidden is that if grocery store "B" shopped at grocery store "A" buying a different list of articles, they could come up with the results that store "B" would be cheaper than store "A." However, the customer only sees that this list of groceries is cheaper at store "A" than store "B"; thus, the person is deceived, and grocery store "A" is rewarded for legally practicing business deception.

The same analysis can be done with other businesses that offer a variety of products.

CONCLUSION

This should serve as a lesson to us. We must not permit ourselves to be sold by the infrastructures of the most important product there is: the Gospel message. Many today are following messengers instead of the message. The words of men are being substituted for the Word of God. Instead of the Church Jesus Christ is building, they are offered an empty form of "Churchianity." Deception is in full swing today and the moment the Church is taken out of the way, darkness will cover the earth and the father of lies will present his deception to the entire world.

Chapter 6

SATAN'S MASTERPIECE

"And the beast which I saw was like unto a leopard, and his feet were as the feet of a bear, and his mouth as the mouth of a lion: and the dragon gave him his power, and his seat, and great authority" (Revelation 13:2).

The key to this chapter is revealed in the above verse with the words, *"...the dragon gave him his power, and his seat, and great authority."* The Antichrist will be inspired by Satan. In other words, he is the recipient of the dragon's power, seat and authority.

We must understand that the dragon, Satan, and the devil are one and the same. This is documented in Revelation 12:9, *"...the great dragon...that old serpent, called the Devil, and Satan, which deceiveth the whole world...."* So when we refer to the serpent, the dragon, Satan, and the devil, we are describing the one who rebelled against the God of creation. He was originally known as "the day star," or the "son of the morning." The King James translators identify him with the name "Lucifer."

THE ANTICHRIST

The Antichrist is considered Satan's masterpiece because he will be fully inspired (or possessed) by him.

The word "antichrist" carries a negative connotation that often leads people to believe that he will appear as one who is in total opposition to the Lord Jesus Christ. In general, Christianity portrays the Antichrist as the most blood-thirsty ruler the world has ever seen. Usually names of tyrannical leaders such as Nero, Napoleon, Stalin and Hitler are mentioned in close proximity to the title of Antichrist.

But it's extremely important to understand that this view is false. Deception does not lie in force, but in falsehood and delusion. Antichrist will deceive people, particularly members of Churchianity, into believing that he is the "real" Christ who has been sent by God.

Therefore, it is imperative to understand that the word "antichrist" means a substitute; he is in place of Christ, an imitation. So it stands to reason that the Antichrist must appear and behave in such a way that he will be confused with the Christ of the Bible. However, this does not mean that such a person lives in an imaginary world. Someone who has been deceived lives in the same world as you and I. Everything from the house you own to the car you drive and the nest egg you have saved is all very much a reality. But the catch occurs when you take these normal facets of life and place them on a new level.

When we talk about deception, we must ask ourselves, "What is our purpose and intent for owning these things?" Furthermore, "How did we come to obtain these material things?" Was it based on our own initiative, or because the government has implemented a system allowing us the opportunity to earn and enjoy these things? Virtually all tax-paying, hard-working, honest citizens would answer the first question with the words, "Comfort and security are the primary goals of my life."

To the second question, the most probable answer would be, "I've worked hard and have taken advantage of the opportunities I have been given." I am convinced that every government wants its citizens to enjoy freedom, prosperity and luxury. That is quite natural, but in the process of offering these goodies and achieving these goals, we detect an underlying spirit that tries to create a peaceful, prosperous world.

What's wrong with that? In and of itself, nothing. Each of us, whether we are a believer or not, takes advantage of the New World Order currently enjoyed particularly in the more prosperous countries of the world. However, if you are a believer, there should be a major distinction between being in the world but not of the world. Jesus made this very clear in Matthew 6:33, *"But seek ye first the kingdom of God, and his righteousness; and all these things shall be added unto you."*

We will now take a further step to analyze something literally out of this world. It can be classified as supernatural and is the work of the great deceiver who desperately seeks to achieve that which can only be accomplished by Jesus Christ, for He is the Prince of peace.

We will learn how spiritual wickedness in high places

cunningly present an alternative to the biblical way of creating a peaceful and prosperous world.

THE GOD OF THE NATIONS

Matthew's gospel account reveals that the devil failed in manipulating Christ to his cause. He offered his glory, power and dominion to Jesus with the words: *"...All these things will I give thee, if thou wilt fall down and worship me"* (Matthew 4:9). This offer reveals a truth that becomes a very painful reality for those who have been swept away by nationalism. This biblical proposition clearly indicates that the devil owns all the kingdoms of this world. Therefore, to assume that certain countries were founded upon God's principles and are under His direct jurisdiction is wrong. As a matter of fact, one of Satan's first and most successful attempts at deception is to tell the nationals that their country is superior to all others. If believers are among those who have fallen for this lie, they are already entangled in Satan's web. As a result, they will have great difficulty in discerning God's prophetic Word. Nationalism will always find its way into their preaching and teaching. Somehow the devil has been successful in intertwining some religious activity—which may sound biblical but is not Christian—into the nation's history. For example, our first president was an occultic Freemason. A majority of the signers of the Declaration of Independence were deists, defined in *Webster's Dictionary* as those who follow "...a system of thoughts advocating natural religion based on human reason rather than revelation." Definitely not Christian! A believer, who also happens to be a nationalist, will not consider this fact, but will continue to follow the dictates of his nation regardless of the truth.

THE GOD OF THIS WORLD

The Bible refers to the devil as the "god of this world." Paul's second letter to the Corinthians warned about those who would reject the glorious Gospel: *"In whom the god of this world hath blinded the minds of them which believe not, lest the light of the glorious gospel of Christ, who is the image of God, should shine unto them"* (2nd Corinthians 4:4). As difficult as it may be to believe, the god of this world is the prince of darkness; subsequently, the entire world lies in obscurity. There is only one exception: the Church of Jesus Christ is the light of the world and diametrically opposes the nations. Therefore, any attempt to unify the Church with national aspirations is not only false, but also conflicts with the foundations of Christianity. Political identities have no direct relation to the Church of Jesus Christ, but to the Christian nationalist. This principle cannot be true for the nationalist because it destroys their pipe dreams of peace and prosperity.

The democratic system of our modern world is just as much under the rule of the prince of darkness as was Hitler's Germany or Stalin's Soviet Union.

As believers, we are fortunate to live in countries where we can openly proclaim the Gospel without fear of government interference. At this point, a majority of countries are opened to the Gospel with varying degrees of limitation, particularly in Communist and Muslim nations.

It is interesting to note that although China has been ruled by a strict communist system which practically outlawed religion, the Church of Jesus Christ is flourishing. A recent statistic from a reliable source states that there are more Christians in China than there are in the United States and Canada combined. This may be true, because the Church of Jesus Christ is not built upon the basis of technology, economy or prosperity, but is founded upon the Rock of salvation and guided by the Holy Spirit. The Spirit has the upper hand when the flesh is subdued.

Our brethren in China, and an array of other countries have suffered immensely for their faith in Jesus, and as a result, the Lord has seen fit to add millions of precious souls to His Church. After all, it is the Lord Jesus who said *"...I will build my church."*

HIS GLOBAL CHURCH

The Lord did not give a special commission or responsibility of building the Church to the first church in Jerusalem, or those that followed. Our Lord transcends all national boundaries, languages, customs, and cultures. The Church is truly global. No specific group of people or nation holds a special position in God's eternal plan of salvation. The true Church is independent of national, racial and cultural boundaries and is exclusively dependent on her head, the Lord Jesus Christ.

For example, God did not give any preference to Turkey even though that was the physical location of the seven churches mentioned in the book of Revelation. Nor did He give any special recognition to Greece even though it was the Greek language that contributed to the preservation of the oldest available manuscripts of the New Testament. Furthermore, the Lord has not ordained or bestowed any authority to the church in Rome, which has become the world's most powerful political/religious entity.

GENTILE DOGS?

I stress these points so that as individual believer you will not become reliant on your nationality in any way. Being proud of your heritage is one thing, but we must never allow that pride to cross boundaries because one has nothing to do with the other.

Addressing the Gentiles in Matthew 15:26, Jesus said, *"...It is not meet to take the children's bread, and to cast it to dogs."* Based on my understanding of Scripture, I have not seen any indication of the Lord apologizing for this statement. Yes, these words seem offensive and are clearly written for everyone to read, however, that statement does not mean that Gentiles are excluded from God's plan of salvation. The Bible says, *"For God so loved the world...."*

Notice the words the Canaanite woman used when she asked Jesus to help her daughter: *"Thou son of David."* Jesus ignored her. Why? Because He was only the son of David to the Jews. When the disciples urged Him, He answered, *"I am not sent but unto the lost sheep of the house of Israel."* The woman heard what Jesus said and addressed Him as "Lord." Her pleading is genuine and she is persistent. To these hurtful words she replied, *"...Truth, Lord: yet the dogs eat of the crumbs which fall from their masters' table."* This woman was free of national, racial, and cultural pride and humbled herself completely in order to get Jesus' attention. How did the Lord reply? *"...O woman, great is thy faith: be it unto thee even as thou wilt. And her daughter was made whole from that very hour"* (Matthew 15:28).

NATIONAL DECEPTION

If you are still not convinced, read what the Lord said about the nations in Isaiah 40:17, *"All nations before him are as nothing; and they are counted to him less than nothing, and vanity."* Not only does He classify the nations as nothing, but they are *"...less than nothing."* So much for the "great nation" theory!

Why is it necessary for us to understand the reality that all nations are subject to the god of this world? Because national deception confuses our understanding of the global position of the Church and Israel. You must become free of the things of this world and focus on spiritual matters, which are heavenly and eternal. When you do, your spiritual eyes will be opened and you will begin to see the glory of heaven and recognize the chaos and confusion of this world. The true Church will always stand opposed to the world.

It should come as no surprise that Israel, God's earthly people, also stand opposed to the nations of the world. Although at this point they are spiritually blind and even enemies of the Gospel according to Romans 11:28, they are, nevertheless, the only nation in the history of the world with the specific promise of a national, collective salvation.

THE FATHER OF LIES

In order to understand Satan, we must examine his intentions. How does he work? What is his goal? Second Corinthians 2:11 says, *"...Lest Satan should get an advantage of us: for we are not ignorant of his devices."* His work is a work of deception and his goal is to replace God the Creator. But because God is the only Creator, the devil is forced into a corner. Masterfully employing his technique of deception, the devil tries to imitate God. The Antichrist is the result, and a near perfect imitation of the Lord Jesus Christ. The Antichrist will be controlled by Satan and will manipulate the world with his trickery to such an extent that the world at large will be convinced beyond a shadow of a doubt that he is God!

When we learn that Satan gives his power, seat, and great authority to the Antichrist, we understand how desperate is his attempt to imitate John 3:35: *"The Father loveth the Son, and hath given all things into his hand"* (John 3:35).

The Father gives all things into the hand of His Son because He *"...loveth the Son."* This love is absent in all the devil's dealings with mankind and his subjects.

Satan does not empower the Antichrist with his authority because he loves him or loves mankind; just the opposite is true: He hates mankind. He is the author of confusion and all of his works and intentions lead to destruction. The ultimate destiny of evil is described in Revelation 20:10, *"And the devil that deceived them was cast into the lake of fire and brimstone, where the beast and the false prophet are, and shall be tormented day and night for ever and ever."*

The opposite of love is hate. God wants all men to be saved and come to the knowledge of the Lord, but Satan tries to hinder the way to salvation by every means available.

THE CLIMAX OF SEDUCTION

The book of Revelation vividly demonstrates the result of this deception. A series of catastrophic events, including a great earthquake and the sun becoming black as sackcloth and the moon as blood will take place after the Lamb opens the sixth seal: *"And the kings of the earth, and the great men, and the rich men, and the chief captains, and the mighty men, and every bondman, and every free man, hid themselves in the dens and in the rocks of the mountains; And said to the mountains and rocks, Fall on us, and hide us from the face of him that sitteth on the throne, and from the wrath of the Lamb: For the great day of his wrath is come; and who shall be able to stand?"* (Revelation 6:15–17). People from all social levels will attempt to hide behind the materials God has created. It's ironic because these people will have completely relied upon the materialistic world. They have lived for materialism up until this point, but now they will experience God's supernatural judgment. Their first impulse will be to escape rather than repent.

MODERN IDOL WORSHIP

If ever there has been a time when man worshipped idols, it is today. I am not talking about idols such as religious icons, but idol worship in the form of materialistic achievements. The more people have, the more they want—larger homes, better cars, more jewelry and bigger investments—all for the sole purpose of pleasing self.

Four more reasons are given in addition to idolatry:

1. Murder
2. Sorcery
3. Fornication
4. Theft

MURDER

When we think about murder, we can't help but consider the millions of unborn babies who are mostly killed for materialistic reasons through the "convenience" of abortion. Although innumerable laws protect human rights, life, property and culture, there is still no law that protects the life of an unborn child. Yet, the Bible proclaims this wonderful truth, *"Thine eyes did see my substance, yet being unperfect; and in thy book all my members were written, which in continuance were fashioned, when as yet there was none of them"* (Psalm 139:16).

It is ironic that the unborn life of a human being is not recognized, but the unborn life of an animal is fanatically defended by animal rights groups. For example, if you found a nest of American bald eagles and threw the eggs you discovered there against the rocks, there is little doubt in my mind that you would be arrested, convicted and imprisoned. Why is it that the murder of an unborn child does not receive the same punishment?

This is one example of the many great successes of the

father of lies. He has convinced humanity at large that man, created in the image of God, has no value and can be destroyed without fear of violating any laws.

We must not neglect to also identify another type of murder of which every one of us stand guilty, *"Whosoever hateth his brother is a murderer..."* (1st John 3:15). It saddens me to say that not only is hate expressed in worldly literature, but is quite frequently found in Christian writings as well. I am particularly referring to political candidates in office. After having seen videos and read books written about many prominent politicians, I have been appalled by the gutter language employed by well-known Christian authors to express their flaming hatred against politicians who are not to their liking.

When we honestly analyze the statement *"Whosoever hateth his brother is a murderer,"* we are all forced to confess guilt. Therefore, the one-sided condemnation of people who have physically murdered someone, or have murdered through the avenue of abortion, does not justify our hating a brother.

SORCERY

The word "sorcery" is translated from the Greek word *pharmakeia* and defined in *Strong's Concordance* as "pharmacy, sorcery, witchcraft." The drug culture in our modern world is well-established and in most cases, well camouflaged. Drugs come in all shapes and forms. Some are available without a prescription and some can only be obtained from a doctor. However, illegal drugs and their related businesses are the main issue in this matter.

Sorcery, witchcraft and magic are all based on deception. Mind-altering drugs also cause deception. Those who consume such drugs are practicing sorcery with their own bodies.

Although we hear a great deal about successful law enforcement battles against illegal drugs, there's no doubt that millions of people will continue in their addiction and remain under the spell of sorcery, which in the form of *pharmakeia,* regardless of its legal status, is at an all-time high.

This type of drug-related sorcery can also be called a lie because it draws users and addicts deeper and deeper into an imaginary world, further away from the truth.

FORNICATION

As we defined previously, the word "fornication" is translated from the Greek word *porneia. Strong's Concordance* defines the word as "adultery, incest, harlotry, unlawful lust." Not only does this include behind-the-counter products, but it applies to our entertainment industry as well. Fornication is glorified in virtually all music. The entertainment industry can no longer afford to delete unseemly activities which constitute fornication from their films and programs because those very activities are what the audience wants to see and hear. The removal of pornography from certain products not only jeopardizes ratings, but also diminishes the attraction of the merchandise.

This point must be emphasized because many of us are quick to accuse the producers of sex-oriented products, when the fact is, the industry only produces what the public demands. As long as an audience is willing to pay for these products, fornication will remain deeply embedded in our society. It is part of our culture today which is evident from the verse we have just read.

What's even more shocking is that pornography is being promoted within Christianity. I was surprised at the volume of pornographic titles available through a Christian mail-order catalog. Usually these titles are camouflaged within promises to strengthen your marriage. So its not surprising that a new statistic reveals that Christian marriages are failing at a faster rate than the marriages of unbelievers.

This assertion prompts the question, "What is pornography?" Pornography can be classified as a third-party intrusion—whether it be a book or movie—into the marriage covenant. The institution of marriage should be limited to the husband and wife. Any type of participation—whether by reading, writing, hearing or seeing—outside of those boundaries constitutes fornication.

THEFT

The sin of theft is not limited to stealing property that belongs to someone else. Theft is a major industry openly practiced all over the world. It includes the theft of ideas, infringement on patents, and of course, the bootlegging of trademark products.

With an ever-fading set of absolutes, it has become extremely difficult to define theft, and, as time goes on, it will become next to impossible. That is one of the many reasons why the insurance business and legal defense system have grown beyond anything imagined only 50 years ago. Our local Yellow Pages sold attorneys enough ads to fill 52 pages, compared with the 16 pages featuring churches.

Many argue that our world has changed for the better. In fact, according to government statistics, our standard of living is at an all-time high and the crime rate has dramatically decreased during the last decade. But that has not changed the heart of man, whose sinful nature continues to break through in various forms. As a result, theft may no longer be as easily detectable as it was years ago.

WRATH OF THE LAMB

In the beginning of this chapter we discussed the wrath of the Lamb documented in Revelation 6:15–17. This is unusual because the last thing that would come to your mind in relation to a lamb is wrath. Our Lord is called the *"...Lamb of God who takes away the sins of the world."* So what does *"...the wrath of the Lamb"* mean? We can easily imagine the wrath of a lion who tears its victims to pieces, but a lamb is a defenseless, tender animal with no intentions of harming anyone.

I believe *"...the wrath of the Lamb"* indicates that man will now see the Lamb of God whom they had rejected. The Lamb who could have saved man will no longer be the Lamb who offers salvation. He will mercilessly expose those who deliberately rebelled against Him. Either the blood of the Lamb has saved you, or the blood of the Lamb will judge you.

It is significant that the Lord will not appear as the Lion of the tribe of Judah. From the fifth chapter of Revelation we know that no one was found worthy to open the seven seals of the book. Then John was told by one of the elders, "...Weep not: behold, the Lion of the tribe of Juda, the Root of David, hath prevailed to open the book, and to loose the seven seals thereof" (verse 5). Clearly, this is Jesus Christ, Son of David, Messiah of Israel and Savior of the world. Based on His royal authority as the Lion of the tribe of Judah, He has the right to open the seals. But as we see in chapter six, the physical opening of the seals will be done by the Lamb, "And I saw when the Lamb opened one of the seals, and I heard, as it were the noise of thunder, one of the four beasts saying, Come and see" (Revelation 6:1).

The opening of the seal will be accomplished through the nature of the Lamb, not the Lion. I believe this is one of the deeper reasons why the people on earth fear the wrath of the Lamb—because it will reveal the victory of the Lamb of God on Calvary's cross. An irreversible eternal defeat will be exposed and the deception will be recognized; however, man will realize it is too late.

It is also significant to mention that these people won't even attempt to repent, even when confronted with the terrifying judgment that has befallen the earth. I believe that is another reason why this is referred to as "...the wrath of the Lamb."

IDOL WORSHIP INSTEAD OF REPENTANCE

A further rejection of the deception is reported in Revelation 9, which occurs after the sixth angel sounds the trumpet resulting in war and the death of a third of mankind. Two of the six billion people who inhabit the earth today will be killed. On a smaller scale, one of every three will die.

How will people react? *"And the rest of the men which were not killed by these plagues yet repented not of the works of their hands, that they should not worship devils, and idols of gold, and silver, and brass, and stone, and of wood: which neither can see, nor hear, nor walk: Neither repented they of their murders, nor of their sorceries, nor of their fornication, nor of their thefts"* (Revelation 9:20–21). They will be worshippers of their own manufactured idols.

FINAL REJECTION

The catastrophe involving the sun will take place at the fourth vial judgment *"...the fourth angel poured out his vial upon the sun; and power was given unto him to scorch men with fire"* (Revelation 16:8). Apparently this is a foretaste of the lake of fire. We cannot even begin to imagine the immense heat that will come upon the earth at that time. It may not be coincidental that a number of scientists claim that a global warming is taking place due to the greenhouse effect. Frankly, I don't believe it. The theory claims that carbon monoxide emission from motor vehicles and industrial-related pollution destroys the ozone shield that protects the earth from damaging ultra-violet sun rays. It is estimated that during the last century, temperatures have risen over 2 degrees Fahrenheit.

The following article appeared in the 1995 January/February issue of *The Futurist:*

Global warming is "The Mother of all environmental scares," according to the late political scientist Aaron Wildavsky. Based on climate computer models, eco-doomsters predict that the Earth's average temperature will increase by 4-9 degrees Fahrenheit over the next century due to the "greenhouse effect."

Burning fossil fuels boosts atmospheric carbon dioxide which traps the sun's heat. What is really happening? The Earth's average temperature has apparently increased by less than a degree (0.9) Fahrenheit in the last century. And here's more bad news for doomsters: Fifteen years of very precise satellite data show that the planet has actually cooled by 0.13 degrees C.

–*The Futurist,* January/February 1995, P.14

The same issue of this publication also revealed some little-published news about the supposed "hole" in the ozone:

In 1992, NASA spooked Americans by declaring that an ozone hole like the one over Antarctica could open up over the United States. *Time* magazine showcased the story on its front cover (February 6, 1992), warning that "danger is shining through the sky...No longer is the threat just to our future; the threat is here and now." Then-Senator Albert Gore thundered in Congress, "We have to tell our children that they must redefine their relationship to the sky as a threatening part of their environment."

What really happened? On April 30, 1992, NASA sheepishly admitted that no ozone hole had opened up over the United States. *Time,* far from trumpeting the news on its cover, buried the admission in four lines of text in its May 11 issue. It's no wonder the American public is frightened.

I believe it is wrong to speculate how this will be fulfilled, especially in light of the fact that many are coming up with their own forced conclusion that industrial development is the cause of the earth's warming.

It is interesting that the next verse clearly reveals that God is the real source of the earth's scorching: *"And men were scorched with great heat, and blasphemed the name of God, which hath power over these plagues: and they repented not to give him glory"* (Revelation 16:9). Its almost unbelievable that these people, who will suffer so immensely, will not repent or give God the glory; instead, they will blaspheme His Name.

The destruction continues: *"And the fifth angel poured out his vial upon the seat of the beast; and his kingdom was full of darkness; and they gnawed their tongues for pain, And blasphemed the God of heaven because of their pains and their sores, and repented not of their deeds"* (Revelation 16:10–11). This defies all logic and understanding. In spite of the sheer terror that will come upon the earth, these people were obviously not scared enough because they still did not repent.

CONCLUSION

I mention these instances from the book of Revelation to drive home the point that deception is not about just making a mistake or following an error; deception includes the spirit, soul and body. These people will have wholeheartedly given themselves to the spirit of lies. They will believe in the success of the Antichrist, his false prophet, and the image of the beast to such an extent that they will refuse to repent. They will not acknowledge their error and will not turn to God.

Chapter 7

THE BEAST, THE FALSE PROPHET AND THE MARK

The subject of this chapter is the three identities highlighted in Revelation 13:

1. The Beast
2. The False Prophet
3. The Mark

We will analyze these three identities and determine who they are, what they do, and what their intentions are.

WHO IS THE BEAST?

The beast is Satan's masterpiece. The deception in which Satan uses so brilliantly to manipulate people into believing that he is the creator is all too successful. That is why the Bible refers to the devil as *"...the god of this world"* and the *"...father of lies."*

The devil's success is evidenced by those outside of faith in Jesus Christ. If you ask someone whether or not they are saved, the answer is often, "Well, you have your religion and I have mine." Many people seem rather content with their decision, so when you tell them that there is only One who saves, they answer, "That's what they all say!" Therefore, it stands to reason that through his deception, Satan must convince people that he is a creator as well.

EVOLUTION

The theoretical "doctrine" of evolution is an extremely successful tool Satan uses to manipulate the masses. If evolution is true, then we are here by sheer accident. If we are here by accident, then we cannot be held responsible for our own actions; there are no absolutes and everything simply evolved from nothing.

While atheists and agnostics generally embrace the theory of evolution as fact, religion, to a certain degree, stands in opposition. Sadly, the theory of evolution has also found its way into religion where it is accepted as scientific fact. However, there remains those who are determined to resist the theory by affirming that creation is the only logical explanation for the existence of life.

It stands to reason that Satan must imitate the Creator and deceive those who believe in creationism but are not born again of the Spirit of God. Part of Satan's strategy targets believers in Christ.

NO LABORATORY PROOF

An overwhelming amount of information circulates on both sides of the evolution/creation argument. If creationism can be scientifically proven in a laboratory, the evolution theory would finally be laid to rest. You can't argue science because it is supposed to be absolute truth; therefore, the average Christian is presented with a problem when faced with the theory of evolution in contrast to the biblical teaching of creationism. How are we to respond?

CREATION IS TO BE UNDERSTOOD BY FAITH

The Bible is our authority; therefore, we look to the Word of God for our answers. We have already established the fact that God created the heavens and the earth, which should be unconditionally believed by all Christians. It is not through science that we prove that the world, and all therein, was created by God.

It is only through His Word, which we have received by faith that we *"...understand that the worlds were framed by the word of God, so that things which are seen were not made of things which do appear"* (Hebrews 11:3).

What is faith? *"Now faith is the substance of things hoped for, the evidence of things not seen"* (Hebrews 11:1). It becomes increasingly obvious that faith is not the substance of humanly contrived science, but of things hoped for, evidenced by things not yet seen.

I have resigned myself to the fact that it is futile to argue with an evolutionist about the creation of this world because they choose to believe in a substitute developed by Satan, the father of lies. It is difficult, if not impossible, to convince someone that his preconceived ideas are wrong. This fact alone exposes our human limitations and glorifies the only One who is able to change the heart and mind. So let us rejoice in the wonderful truth that God created the heavens and the earth; He is the beginning and the end; and He is the author and finisher of our salvation. He is also the

One who guarantees that He will build His Church!

We should not become overly-concerned with political and social movements whose efforts lie in trying to hinder the work of the Church. The Church of Jesus Christ cannot be destroyed. Praise God when persecutions take place, because through them the Church will grow even stronger. The Church is an eternal creation. Don't be afraid when people try to instill fear in you, or when things are not going well in the world around you.

It is no secret that Bible-believing Christians do not speak, act, or preach a "politically correct" philosophy. We discriminate against the doctrines taught in other religions, and we boldly declare that there is only one Name under heaven given among men to be saved, and that is the name of Jesus. Today's general consensus is that "all are good; just name your own god and if that works for you, that's great." However, the message of the Bible does not leave any room for deviation; Jesus Christ alone saves sinners!

SATANIC TRINITY

Satan is the great imitator. As believers, we are united with Jesus, we are His Body and we are one. Satan tries to achieve the same unity through the cooperation of the beast, the false prophet, and the use of the mark. Each serves to solidify Satan's consolidated world.

We are not ignorant of Satan's devices; we understand his purpose. He is building a great global world of peace and prosperity; the great imitation. Consequently, with the exception of the elect, he will deceive all mankind.

It should not come as any surprise that Scripture reveals a satanic trinity documented in Revelation 16:13, *"And I saw three unclean spirits like frogs come out of the mouth of the dragon, and out of the mouth of the beast, and out of the mouth of the false prophet."*

The dragon imitates the Father, the beast imitates the Son, and the false prophet imitates the Spirit of God.

What is their intention? *"For they are the spirits of devils, working miracles, which go forth unto the kings of the earth and of the whole world, to gather them to the battle of that great day of God Almighty"* (Revelation 16:14). It is important to emphasize that the entire world is involved. This line of thought corresponds with Psalm 2:1–2, *"Why do the heathen rage, and the people imagine a vain thing? The kings of the earth set themselves, and the rulers take counsel together, against the LORD, and against his anointed...."* It doesn't matter where you live or what form of government rules your country, all are represented by *"...the kings of the earth."*

WHY IS THE ANTICHRIST CALLED THE BEAST?

The word "beast" can be defined as an animal. Martin Luther uses the word "animal" in his translation of the Bible. After God created the world, separated light from darkness and water from land, and created vegetation and animals, *"...God said, Let us make man in our image, after our likeness..."* (Genesis 1:26). The previous verse describes the creation of animals, *"And God made the beast of the earth after his kind, and cattle after their kind, and every thing that creepeth upon the earth after his kind: and*

God saw that it was good" (verse 25). A distinction is made between the animal world which He created *"...after their kind..."* in their unique and peculiar likeness, and God's creation of man *"...in our image after our likeness...."* Only man is created in God's image!

What is man's position according to God's plan? Man is to *"...have dominion over the fish of the sea, and over the fowl of the air, and over the cattle, and over all the earth, and over every creeping thing that creepeth upon the earth..."* (verse 26).

The Antichrist is called the beast simply because he has lost the right to be included with those who are created in God's image. The Antichrist is a product of Satan, but is not actually Satan. If Satan is not the Antichrist, then who is he? In Revelation 12:9 he is described as, *"...the great dragon...that old serpent, called the Devil, and Satan...."* He is the originator of sin who now empowers the beast to do his bidding: *"And I stood upon the sand of the sea, and saw a beast rise up out of the sea, having seven heads and ten horns, and upon his horns ten crowns, and upon his heads the name of blasphemy"* (Revelation 13:1). Imagine the sight: a beast with seven heads and ten horns coming out of the sea!

John continues to describe the likeness of this beast, *"And the beast which I saw was like unto a leopard, and his feet were as the feet of a bear, and his mouth as the mouth of a lion...."* (Revelation 13:2). Three animals illustrate the appearance of this beast.

The verse continues, *"...the dragon gave him his power, and his seat, and great authority."* The mystery is revealed;

the Antichrist is not Satan, yet he receives power, position, and authority from the dragon who is Satan.

I believe these characteristics—seven heads, ten horns, the likeness of a leopard, bear and lion—are spiritual characteristics, and should not to be viewed as physical traits. However, these characteristics earn the Antichrist the title of "beast" or "animal." No longer does he resemble a human being created in the image of God.

Galatians 5:22 outlines the differences between animal and man: *"But the fruit of the Spirit is love, joy, peace, longsuffering, gentleness, goodness, faith, meekness, temperance; against such there is no law."* An animal does not possess these characteristics, nor the capabilities of using such gifts. The beast goes against everything that is of God and, by nature, everything that was intended for us to receive from God.

SATAN'S ORIGIN

To better determine the origin of sin, we must further investigate Satan, the power behind the Antichrist. Isaiah 14 offers a historic view of sin's origin: *"How art thou fallen from heaven, O Lucifer, son of the morning! how art thou cut down to the ground, which didst weaken the nations! For thou hast said in thine heart, I will ascend into heaven, I will exalt my throne above the stars of God: I will sit also upon the mount of the congregation, in the sides of the north: I will ascend above the heights of the clouds; I will be like the most High"* (Isaiah 14:12–14). This passage explains the downfall of this mighty heavenly angel. At some moment in time, the idea of rebellion was born in the heart of the "son of the morning," which resulted in the origin of sin.

Notice that the words, "I will" are used five times in verses 13 and 14:

1. *...I will ascend into heaven...*
2. *...I will exalt my throne above the stars of God...*
3. *...I will sit upon the mount of the congregation...*
4. *...I will ascend above the heights of the clouds...*
5. *...I will be like the most High...*

Obviously Satan was dissatisfied with his position of grandeur as a beautiful being and coveted God's position as Most High. When we think about all of the false teachers and religions which preach that this is an obtainable goal, it seems as though time has stood still since the idea was first conceived.

EQUALITY TO GOD

Satan's primary intentions of desiring equality with God are unmistakable. Another example of sin's origin can be found in Ezekiel 28, where we read this fascinating description, *"Son of man, take up a lamentation upon the king of Tyrus, and say unto him, Thus saith the Lord GOD; Thou sealest up the sum, full of wisdom, and perfect in beauty"* (verse 12). Although this is addressed to the king of Tyrus, we know that Satan stands behind it. How do we know? Because the king of Tyrus was never *"...full of wisdom"* or *"...perfect in beauty."*

Another example is seen when Jesus said to Peter, *"Get thee behind me, Satan,"* (Matthew 16:23). Peter did not actually become Satan; however, his words could be considered satanic. Peter had just confessed, *"...Thou art the Christ, the Son of the living God."* Jesus revealed the origin of Peter's statement in verse 17: *"...flesh and blood hath not revealed it unto thee, but my Father which is in heaven."* Peter's first statement originated with God the Father, but his second statement, *"...Be it far from thee, Lord,"* which was directed against the cross, originated with Satan.

The transferal of the spirit of Satan upon the king of Tyrus is evident, *"Thou hast been in Eden the garden of God; every precious stone was thy covering, the sardius, topaz, and the diamond, the beryl, the onyx, and the jasper, the sapphire, the emerald, and the carbuncle, and gold: the workmanship of thy tabrets and of thy pipes was prepared in thee in the day that thou wast created. Thou art the anointed cherub that covereth; and I have set thee so: thou wast upon the holy mountain of God; thou hast walked up and down in the midst of the stones of fire. Thou wast perfect in thy ways from the day that thou wast created, till iniquity was found in thee"* (Ezekiel 28:13–15). The king of Tyrus was not perfect, and we can safely say that he was never in the Garden of Eden.

It is important to remember that we must identify who is being spoken about when we read Bible prophecy. In doing so, we learn to separate these two facts: God is the Creator of heaven and earth and Satan is the deceiver who tries to imitate God. Satan wants all men to be lost; however, God's intention is for all men to be saved. This process has been going on for almost 6,000 years.

Incidentally, that was the point of contact when Satan deceived Eve in the Garden of Eden with the words, *"...ye shall be as gods."* Satan offered an equality that he himself did not even possess, to God's crown of creation; man.

MODERN EQUALITY

The philosophy of equality is nothing more than man's ridiculous attempt to become God. After all, no one in their right mind would claim to be God or consider himself equal to Him...or would they? Sadly, this idea is not as far-fetched as we may think. Egalitarian philosophy is taught all over the world. For instance, equality became the key word and foundation for the Communist Revolution. At that time, the peasants were rebelling against the aristocrats, or, in today's vernacular, the employees were fighting for an equal share of benefits with the employers.

Communism proclaimed that it would create a "workers paradise" on earth by eliminating those considered to be in the way: aristocrats, business people, intellectuals, etc. The end result was made visible to the entire world when the Soviet Union collapsed in bankruptcy. However, that was not the end of Satan's egalitarian philosophy; the process continues unabated.

One of the principles on which the United States was founded is that all men are created equal. This can be interpreted in many different ways, but does not change the fact that the principle is false. For example, I am not equal to my wife. We are distinctly different, not only in physical appearance but in emotional qualities as well. A father usually takes on the role of disciplinarian in raising children. When it comes time to punish the child, a mother will usually interfere and plead a case for leniency. Many other characteristics illustrate the differences between male and female. Notice that the Bible does not say that God created male and female "both in His image"; rather, *"...in the image of God, created he him male and female created he them."* We may also add that man was created out of the dust of the ground and woman was created from man's body. The two were definitely not created equal.

In fact, God made the following command to Israel regarding their mode of dress: *"The woman shall not wear that which pertaineth unto a man, neither shall a man put on a woman's garment: for all that do so are abomination unto the LORD thy God"* (Deuteronomy 22:5).

GLOBALISM AND EQUALITY

This godly segregation is not limited to a husband and wife, but extends to the Church and the nations. The spirit of globalism is successfully erasing the languages and borders of the nations. This form of global deception is irreversible.

For example, every one of us, particularly in the western world, depend on globalism. Whether we are purchasing a new car or shopping for clothing, we are actively supporting globalism.

If you need further proof, read the business section of your local newspaper and notice how many companies are merging today. Large companies are jockeying for a position with global proportions. For example, the merger of German car manufacturer Mercedes Benz with the American Chrysler Company vividly demonstrate the success of globalism. Is the corporation now considered German or American? There is no precise answer. It is clear to see that today's global economy is erasing national boundaries. Unity is being established in politics, economy, finance and religion.

CHRISTIANS AND GLOBALISM

A number of evangelists, churches, and Christian ministries have publicly declared their attempt to "Christianize" the United States. One of the most visible organizations is the Christian Coalition. It is not my intention to criticize this, or any other movement, for the valid concerns they present to the government; however, I do feel it is necessary to point out that the vast majority of evangelical Christians are too deeply involved in the political and social processes of the United States. The common factor found in most of these organizations can be summarized with one word: Americanism. When Pat Buchanan announced his candidacy under the Republican Party to run for President of the United States, Liberty University published a poll revealing that over 80% of its students would vote for him. One of the reasons cited was his opposition to globalism. This revelation demonstrates that these young Christians were being educated by professors whose philosophies were based on anti-globalism.

One often-repeated phrase among political candidates has been "American job security." All Americans—and every citizen of every country, for that matter—would obviously endorse their own country by giving it first priority when it comes to jobs. However, many people overlook the fact that the United States has harvested more jobs from other countries in recent history than ever before. Voices in Europe are now being heard against the exportation of jobs to the United States because of cheap labor. If jobs were the real issue, then globalism has performed its greatest service to the anti-globalist.

I mention this instance not because of my political preference, but rather to show that globalism is not a matter of choice; it is the result of an evolutionary, sociological process.

A recent article published in *Midnight Call* magazine revealed that four out of five new jobs in the United States are created by foreign firms. Europeans in general, and Swiss, German, Belgium and Dutch in particular, have the highest labor cost in the world. The present exchange rate indicates that one manufacturing hour in Europe costs approximately 25% more than the United States. The average work week now stands at 36 1/2 hours compared to 47 3/4 hours in the United States. Retirement age for employees in several European countries has been lowered to 62, while it is being raised beyond 65 in the United States.

YOU CAN'T ARGUE SUCCESS

Globalism is here to stay, and will proceed at a more accelerated pace in the near future. There may be setbacks, along with a temporary return to nationalism in various countries; however, based on the prophetic

Word, the world in general must continue to join together in order to fulfill Satan's desire to create a unified world where all people are equal and live together in peace and prosperity. That is the great deception! Unity spells success and against success there is no argument. It will lead to the point at which *"...all the world wondered after the beast."* The epitome of his deception is described in Revelation 13:8, *"And all that dwell upon the earth shall worship him...."*

Subsequently, it is ridiculous to think that any action by a certain group or nation can reverse this process. Ultimately Christians will be disappointed to see that their time, energy, and finances have been wasted. As a result, they will realize that their attempts were destined to fail. Had they heeded the Word of God, they would have known that Jesus said, *"...My kingdom is not of this world: if my kingdom were of this world, then would my servants fight..."* (John 18:36). No matter how justified a social action or reaction to various injustices may seem, the Church has not been called to get involved. Our task is, and will always remain the same, *"...Go ye into all the world, and preach the gospel to every creature"* (Mark 16:15).

THE "YOU ARE GOD" DECEPTION

Renowned author and apologist Dave Hunt has exposed a great number of popular teachers who openly preach, "You are God, act like God." That is a very dangerous teaching. Who was the God who became flesh? The Lord Jesus Christ. The false teaching that claims you can actually be God seems to overlook that, *"He is despised and rejected... and we esteemed him not."* The Scripture continues to describe God in the flesh, *"...a man of sorrows, and acquainted with grief: and we hid as it were our faces from him; he was despised, and we esteemed him not"* (Isaiah 53:3). The Bible leaves absolutely no room for glorying in the flesh; therefore, we must conclude that those teachers who proclaim the need for self-glorification, self-love and self-esteem are preaching another gospel. Do you want to follow Jesus or do you want to follow the one who says, "I am the great one, I will exalt my throne above the stars and I will be like God?"

GOD BECAME MAN, BUT MAN CANNOT BECOME GOD

Following Jesus means to walk the narrow path. It also means you understand that your time on this earth is limited and you are just passing through. The Bible says, *"...teach us to number our days, that we may apply our hearts unto wisdom"* (Psalm 90:12). Many of us reading these lines will not be here at this time next year because every one of us has an appointment with death. Our physical beings are temporary tabernacles with no future or promise. The older we get, the more we seem to notice. My philosophy on aging goes something like this: you're over the hill at 40, you know it at 50, you feel it at 60, you can't deny it at 70, and you brag about your age at 80.

If your faith is anchored in Him, who is the Word from the beginning, then you have a wonderful future to look forward to. Let's submit ourselves to Him who did the will of God; the Lord Jesus Christ.

THE ANTICHRIST'S POWER OF DECEPTION

The Antichrist will rise to power by means of deception through the powers made available to him by the dragon. But how will he accomplish it? In the same way a politician is elected, he will promote himself and make prospective voters believe that his election will solve most of their problems. The Antichrist will be extremely successful and the result will be that, *"...all the world wondered after the beast"* (Revelation 13:3).

The Antichrist's rise to power in the person of the beast is described in Daniel 11:21–24, *"And in his estate shall stand up a vile person, to whom they shall not give the honour of the kingdom: but he shall come in peaceably, and obtain the kingdom by flatteries. And with the arms of a flood shall they be overthrown from before him, and shall be broken; yea, also the prince of the covenant. And after the league made with him he shall work deceitfully: for he shall come up, and shall become strong with a small people. He shall enter peaceably...."* This description is quite significant. Doesn't it remind you of today's politicians? Don't they come in *"peaceably,"* manipulate with *"flatteries,"* and work *"deceitfully?"* The fundamentals of democratic philosophy require a candidate to say what pleases potential voters in order to obtain public confidence and votes. But the bottom line is deception.

Jesus' response to the disciples' regarding the endtimes should not come as a surprise: *"...Take heed that no man deceive you*" (Matthew 24:4). The terrible thing about deception is that those who are being deceived don't even know it. They may think they are acting in accordance to God's Word and believe what is right, yet they are in complete darkness. That is the work of the master deceiver, the father of lies, Satan and his protege the beast. The Bible says, "*...and all the world wondered after the beast.*" Ultimately, the entire world will follow the Satan-inspired beast.

Chapter 8

THE "OTHER" BEAST

Accerding to Scripture we know that the first beast comes from "out of the sea." On the other hand, the false prophet, or *"other beast"* comes from out of the earth. These two unique identities serve the same purpose.

We believe that the first beast emerges as an unknown person from out of the sea of nations. For that reason, I reject all speculations regarding the Antichrist's identity. It has been said that certain popes might fit the criteria of the Antichrist. It has also been suggested that Hitler, Mussolini, and Stalin could have been the Antichrist. One popular preacher even insisted that Juan Carlos, King of Spain, was the Antichrist. So why is it that Christians waste their time by trying to identify a character whom the Bible specifically says will not be revealed until the light of the world has been removed? The Church is the light of the world, and is a point Paul clarifies in 2nd Thessalonians 2:6, *"...now ye know what withholdeth that he might be revealed in his time."*

There's no doubt that Hitler was a forerunner of the beast; he came from out of nowhere. Think about it for a moment: Hitler entered Germany as a foreigner, an unknown painter who possessed absolutely no credentials. Suddenly, through his cunning devices, he deceived a nation considered intellectually advanced. Just recently I heard a statistic that claimed 47% of the physicians in Germany were members of the Nazi party. These doctors who studied for many years were obviously well-educated, but willingly supported Hitler's philosophy. They possessed the intellect to analyze Adolf Hitler's intent, but they couldn't use it because they, too, were deceived.

The Antichrist is not going to appear as a bad guy with blood trickling down the corners of his mouth; instead, he'll be the nicest guy we'd ever want to meet! The Antichrist's popularity will be the primary work of the "other" beast, the false prophet who promotes the Antichrist. The Bible reveals that these two identities will work hand in hand to create an image in the mind of the world's population: that the Messiah promised in virtually all religions has come. That will be the Antichrist.

CAUTION: BEAST AT WORK

Deception is the promotion of a willful belief in something that is not real. It is not brought about by force, but by subtle manipulation and trickery. The beast will use deception because he seeks self-glorification. We already saw that Satan sought to be glorified as God in Isaiah 14. Second Thessalonians 2:4 says, "...*Who opposeth and exalteth himself above all that is called God, or that is worshipped; so that he as God sitteth in the temple of God, shewing himself that he is God."* Satan wants the same honor due only to the Lord Jesus Christ.

This imitation is in full swing today. Just visit your local Christian bookstore and you will notice a variety of prominently displayed books having absolutely nothing to do with Christianity. These books are offered, praised and endorsed as good, solid, theological books. Deception within Christianity is undeniable.

FIRST DECEPTION

Let us return to the Garden of Eden where it all began. In the form of a serpent, Satan was already at work in Genesis 3:4–5, *"And the serpent said unto the woman, Ye shall not surely die: For God doth know that in the day ye eat thereof, then your eyes shall be opened, and ye shall be as gods, knowing good and evil."* Notice how the devil wraps the truth in a bunch of lies. He was telling the truth when he said, *"...ye shall be as gods"* because in verse 22 we read, *"...the LORD God said, Behold, the man is become as one of us, to know good and evil...."* However, truth turns to deceipt when he adds the words, *"...ye shall not surely die."* In like manner, Satan doesn't mind if we believe a little bit of the truth, but he will never present the whole truth. We will find a little bit of truth disguised in every false teaching. If you start to believe it, the devil will have you believing all kinds of lies.

STANDING IN FAITH

How can we protect ourselves in these endtimes and remain grounded in, and fully convinced of the truth? By staying in God's Word, which is truth! Satan does not want us to have fellowship with God, nor does he want us to read His Word. Satan is victorious when our priorities change and our relationship with God is not number one.

We are not expected to wage a battle against the devil, but we are expected to stand still in faith. Some preachers teach that we should fight back when Satan launches various attacks. If we do this we are fighting a losing battle.

HOW TO STAND

The Bible's advice to us is this: *"Put on the whole armour of God, that ye may be able to stand against the wiles of the devil...Wherefore take unto you the whole armour of God, that ye may be able to withstand in the evil day, and having done all, to stand. Stand therefore, having your loins girt about with truth, and having on the breastplate of righteousness"* (Ephesians 6:11,13,14). The devil is powerless when a believer has a right relationship and constant communion with Christ. James 4:7 says, *"...Resist the devil, and he will flee from you."*

Sometimes I hear someone in a prayer meeting say, "Oh Lord, help me overcome this temptation." A child of God praying to the Lord to overcome a certain habit may sound wonderful, but I'm sorry to inform you that it just won't happen. Why not? Because Jesus already overcame for us 2,000 years ago on Calvary's cross when He cried out *"...It is finished."* In most cases, the person who prays that prayer really doesn't want to give up that sinful habit or passion. This often leads to the next step, which is even more dangerous: "I prayed about it, but the Lord hasn't taken it away from me." In other words, it's the Lord's fault!

We can't reverse the succession of Scripture's clear instruction: *"...Resist the devil and he will flee from you."* The passage doesn't say anything about fighting or opposing the devil; it simply says to resist him. In other words, just say "no" to sin. When we are consistent in saying "no," the devil will flee from us. God knows our heart, mind, thoughts and intentions. Verse 8 says, *"Draw nigh to God, and he will draw nigh to you. Cleanse your hands, ye sinners; and purify your hearts, ye double minded"* (James 4:8). If we stay in the truth at all times and at all costs, we will experience continuous victory in our life in Christ. We don't have to be fearful of anything, *"...If God be for us, who can be against us?"* (Romans 8:31).

WHO IS THE FALSE PROPHET?

Before we identify the false prophet, it is important to highlight the difference between the "first beast" and the "other beast." Revelation 13:5 says, *"And there was given unto him a mouth speaking great things and blasphemies; and power was given unto him...And it was given unto him to make war with the saints, and to overcome them: and power was given him over all kindreds, and tongues, and nations"* (verses 5,7). Did you notice that the "first beast" is a poor fellow who apparently has nothing because everything has been given to him? He may be somebody with a new idea, a political philosophy under the auspice and authority of the free world who will bring forth a new system so fantastic that no one will be able to deny his success. But only those with spiritually discerning ears can already hear his footsteps today. I don't know who he is, but I can assure you that his spirit is at work today.

A LAMB WITH TWO HORNS

What does the Bible say about this false prophet? He is described in Revelation 13:11, *"And I beheld another beast coming up out of the earth; and he had two horns like a lamb, and he spake as a dragon."* Is it possible that these *"...two horns like a lamb"* could be an imitation of the Lamb of God? Horns symbolize power, but in this context it is presented in the likeness of a lamb. Not the *"...Lamb as it had been slain,"* in Revelation 5:6 describing the Lord, but this lamb-like creature that prominently displays power (two horns) and speaks like a dragon.

RELIGION AND ECONOMY

These two horns undoubtedly represent the religious and economic power structures which currently rule the world. Economy has overtaken politics. Government and political leaders can no longer decide the success or failure of the economy. They certainly can help it along by maneuvering certain laws that would assist in its growth, but that is the extent of it. For example, the United States cannot afford to offend China politically because of the economy. Some analysts suggest that China will develop into the greatest world market in several decades. American guidelines in regard to communist China were sacrificed for the sake of economy. The military strength of the former Soviet Union, the United States and Europe has been drastically reduced since the fall of communism. It has become extremely difficult for any government to increase the budget for defense because of economy.

Religion has been reintroduced as a necessary power-broker in a civilized society. When you read the entire description of the false prophet, you can't help but tremble at the magnitude of deception coming over the world. Billions of people will wholeheartedly support the new global, social, democratic system. Woe unto those who oppose it.

Continuing in verse 12 we read, *"...he exerciseth all the power of the first beast before him, and causeth the earth and them which dwell therein to worship the first beast, whose deadly wound was healed."* It is important to reiterate that the Antichrist, identified as the beast who rises out of the sea, is a newcomer, an unknown with no power or authority in and of himself. Everything he possesses has been received directly from the dragon, whom we identified as Satan: *"...and the dragon gave him his power, and his seat, and great authority...And they worshipped the dragon which gave power unto the beast...And there was given unto him a mouth speaking great things and blasphemies; and power was given unto him to continue forty and two months...And it was given unto him to make war with the saints...and power was given him over all kindreds, and tongues, and nations"* (verses 2,4,5,7). This beast is the devil incarnate; he is the one for whom those whose names were not written in the Lamb's Book of Life have been waiting.

PERSONALITY CULTS

Some may say, "We now live in a democratic world where no one would endorse a dictatorship!" This may be true for individual nations; however, on a global scale, we are being indoctrinated to expect a world leader. Just read your daily newspaper and notice how sports celebrities are revered; one hall of fame after another is being established, and movie stars are idolized. It is significant that they are called "stars" because Lucifer is also described as the "fallen star" and the "son of the morning." Politicians are wholeheartedly supported by their constituencies as though they were gods.

It is certainly not too far-fetched to assume that when someone actually does come on the scene performing miracles in the sight of all people, that person will be worshipped as God.

The world at large is crying out for someone different, someone who can take charge of the problems of this world and solve them.

POWER OF THE FALSE PROPHET

The "other beast" will come out of the earth and exercise all the power of the first beast. That means he won't need to be given power because he will already possess it: "...*he exerciseth all the power of the first beast before him, and causeth the earth and them which dwell therein to worship the first beast, whose deadly wound was healed. And he doeth great wonders, so that he maketh fire come down from heaven on the earth in the sight of men, And deceiveth them that dwell on the earth by the means of those miracles which he had power to do in the sight of the beast; saying to them that dwell on the earth, that they should make an image to the beast, which had the wound by a sword, and did live"* (Revelation 13:12–14). This will be another amazing world leader who has power in his own right and endorses the Antichrist.

POWER OF RELIGION

There's no doubt the false prophet personifies the religious aspect of this power structure. We already discussed the fact that he appears in the likeness of a lamb with two horns symbolizing the powers which I understand to be two-fold; economy and religion.

What does he do with his power? *"...he...causeth the earth and them which dwell therein to worship the first beast..."*(verse 12). He is not the Antichrist, but he will become a voluntary promoter. We can think of him in terms of being the Antichrist's public relations director.

This amazing man will publicly demonstrate his power so that there will be no question about the authority he possesses: *"...he doeth great wonders...he maketh fire come down from heaven on the earth in the sight of men."*

Remember, it was Elijah who was given the power to make fire come out of heaven and devour the enemies. Later on, the disciples asked the Lord to do the same against their perceived enemies. Satan's imitation via the false prophet will show the world that he is one of the two prophets expected to come to earth.

ECONOMIC GLOBALISM

We have spoken about globalism and have seen how the world is increasingly being unified. For example, from the dozens of car manufacturers that existed only 60 years ago, only two remain in the United States. However, these two are not limited to one country; they literally operate on all five continents. This also holds true for Japanese, German, French, Italian and Korean car manufacturers. No longer does Britain independantly manufacture cars.

As far as the aeronautics industry is concerned, with the exception of Russia, only two conglomerates remain: American Boeing and European Airbus Company.

A social, democratic, capital-based society can only function properly when there is room for competition. Therefore, it is only natural to wonder whether there will even be any competition in the future. I believe that question can only be answered hypothetically. The economy is as unpredictable as politics or the weather; however, we know from Scripture that a one-world power structure will develop and final authority will be instituted when the Antichrist, supported by the false prophet, rules the world.

MILITARY

On the military level, we witnessed the Soviet Union and United States arming themselves until they finally came to the realization that the result would be mutual destruction; subsequently, there is a drastic decrease in today's military. Although weapons are still being manufactured and sold, the entire weapons industry has been substantially reduced. We can only imagine what will transpire when global manufacturing giants face each other; someone will have to step in and play referee. That someone may very well be the Antichrist.

MEDIA SUCCESS

Not only will the Antichrist have amazing diplomatic skills and a huge following, but he will also demonstrate to the world that he is divine as well as human. The media will report to all nations that this miracle worker is for real; he is God and he has the power to prove it. But it is vitally important to remember that it all adds up to deception. In verse 14 we read, *"...And deceiveth them that dwell on the earth by the means of those miracles which he had power to do...."* Remember, deception involves believing in something that is not true. Ultimately, we have two choices: either to believe the truth, or believe a lie!

LYING SIGNS AND WONDERS

When Paul refers to the Antichrist in 2nd Thessalonians 2:9, he writes, *"...Even him, whose coming is after the working of Satan with all power and signs and lying wonders."* The Antichrist is the product of Satan and will come with power, signs, and wonders. Notice that the Bible describes them as *"...lying wonders."* This is a key element of deception. For the most part, people only believe what they can see. Some people don't believe in God because they can't see Him; therefore, they leave themselves open to Satan's mastery and will believe his signs and wonders.

The Antichrist will successfully deceive people,

"...*because they received not the love of the truth, that they might be saved*" (verse 10). This verse reveals the fact that everyone has the ability to either say "yes" to the truth or "yes" to a lie. In this case, the people have made up their minds to believe the lie.

Paul continues, "*And for this cause God shall send them strong delusion, that they should believe a lie*" (verse 11). What a shocking statement! For 2,000 years, God in His mercy has allowed the proclamation of the Gospel all over the world: "*...Believe on the Lord Jesus Christ, and thou shalt be saved....*" Collectively, man will refuse to believe the truth, opting to believe the lie. Verse 12 continues, "*...That they all might be damned who believed not the truth, but had pleasure in unrighteousness.*"

Chapter 9

THE IMAGE

I n order to successfully implement global authority, it will not be enough for the world to worship Satan and the beast because there will always be those who do not fall in line. The false prophet has it figured out and will give an order, *"...saying to them that dwell on the earth that they should make an image to the beast...."* This will be the central focus of the entire world.

We know that the world's most powerful religions are centered on an object. The Muslims have their black rock in Mecca and Catholics have the Vatican in Rome. Religions lacking a tangible object are not found very attractive. One of the reasons Mormonism is so appealing, and increasing in number and power is because they have built some of the most beautiful temples.

WHAT IS THE IMAGE OF THE BEAST?

We don't really know what this image will consist of, but it stands to reason that computers will be involved. The computer can receive, store, and retrieve information from anyone living on planet Earth. The computer is able to dispense this information to any place and at any time.

A computer can make the Antichrist, the false prophet and his lying signs and wonders visible to the whole world via the television.

This manufactured image of the beast will be controlled by the false prophet, *"...he had power to give life unto the image of the beast...."* Believers know that only God has the power to give life, but here we see that the false prophet will *"...give life"* to a manufactured system, which we can presume to be the software.

Our computers may still be far from having life; however, computer scientists forecast that in the future, man may be "married" to machines.

Presently, I am reading a book entitled, *Spiritual Machines* and quite frankly, I am astonished at the progress computer scientists have made thus far. Important to note is that this method of technology is not static, but is multiplying itself in astronomical proportions. What's new today is outdated within a matter of only a few months, sometimes even only weeks. Most of us don't fully realize our dependence on man-made equipment, particularly the computer. An otherwise simple transaction such as cashing your check at the bank is virtually impossible without the use of a computer. Some of the things I have read in trade publications dealing with future computer science frightfully reveal the tendency toward man's integration with machine.

THE AUTHORITY OF THE IMAGE

What will this image do? The Bible says *"...the image of the beast should both speak and cause that as many as would not worship the image of the beast should be killed."* We must take careful notice of the fact that the image of the beast will now be the authority and will no longer be in the hands of the false prophet or the Antichrist. It is the image of the beast that will cause those who do not worship to be killed.

Is that possible? At this time, we would classify such a statement as science fiction, but will it still be considered fiction a few years from now? Is it possible to manufacture a machine that can know what we think, or in this case, identify whether or not we are worshipping the image of the beast? I am fully convinced that the technology already exists and could be implemented at any time to perform such a task. This fact clearly reveals the religious aspect: Life will then depend on whether or not we worship the image of the beast.

POWER OF ECONOMY

We identified the lamb's second horn as representing economy, and once again we turn to Revelation 13:16–17 for a fuller explanation, *"And he causeth all, both small and great, rich and poor, free and bond, to receive a mark in their right hand, or in their foreheads: And that no man might buy or sell, save he that had the mark, or the name of the beast, or the number of his name."* This is a complete, global, economic monopoly; no one will be able to exist without buying or selling.

The world will conclude that this is the best system, and for the first time in human history, crime will be abolished, tax fraud eliminated and absolutely no secrecy will be tolerated. Every soul on the face of the earth will be integrated into the final, global, economic system that promises perpetual peace and prosperity for all. That, dear friend, is the great deception presently taking place all over the world.

POWER OF NATIONALISM

One of the most hidden deceptions which I must not fail to stress at the conclusion of this chapter is national deception. I have spoken to a number of people in various geographical locations and noticed that mostly everyone believes that his government and nation is different from all others. Tens of millions of Christians are involved in some type of political activism without really knowing the truth behind it. That is just another form of deception because the Bible does not leave room for the Church's political involvement in any country. The Church consists of born again believers, elect from among all the nations of the world who are, in fact, subject to the government of their respective nations, but who have not been given any special promises regarding their particular nation. Therefore, we must reiterate that every nation is subject to the god of this world.

No matter how much we would like to believe that our nation was founded on biblical principles, it does not line up with what the Bible actually teaches. The great temptation is recorded in Matthew 4: *"...the devil taketh him (Jesus) up into an exceeding high mountain, and sheweth him all the kingdoms of the world, and the glory of them; And saith unto him, All these things will I give thee, if thou wilt fall down and worship me"* (verses 8–9). The devil offered all the nations of the world to the Son of God, revealing that he is in fact their ruler. After all, you can't give something away that you don't own in the first place. This confirms that all nations, regardless of government or rule, constitute the kingdom of darkness ruled by the god of this world. Therefore, if we choose to fight for our "Christian" rights in our nation, we fight a losing battle.

Although Satan rules the world, this planet and the entire universe belongs to Him who created it, one day Jesus will reveal His undisputed rulership, at which time, every knee shall bow and every tongue confess that Jesus Christ is Lord!

THE TWO PROPHETS

The only voice of protest will be heard from the two witnesses of God in the city of Jerusalem. But ultimately, they, too, will be overcome: *"And when they shall have finished their testimony, the beast that ascendeth out of the bottomless pit shall make war against them, and shall overcome them, and kill them. And their dead bodies shall lie in the street of the great city, which spiritually is called Sodom and Egypt, where also our Lord was crucified"* (Revelation 11:7–8). As a result of their death, a global Christmas party will take place: *"And they that dwell upon the earth shall rejoice over them, and make merry, and shall send gifts one to another; because these two prophets tormented them that dwelt on the earth"* (verse 10). This verse clearly demonstrates just how effective the deception of the beast, the false prophet, and the mark will really be.

The truth these two prophets proclaim will be considered torment because people will hate the truth. This is a fulfillment of 2nd Thessalonians 2:11 which says, *"And for this cause God shall send them strong delusion, that they should believe a lie."* However, the remarkable success of the beast, false prophet and mark will only be temporary. The end will occur when the Jewish Messiah, the Lord Jesus Christ comes with great power and glory to the land of Israel and His feet stand on the Mount of Olives, *"And then shall that Wicked be revealed, whom the Lord shall consume, with the spirit of his mouth, and shall destroy with the brightness of his coming"* (2nd Thessalonians 2:8).

SUMMARY

The beast, false prophet, and the mark will come on the world scene as a product of Satan's inspiration. These three identities will successfully implement the greatest Gentile power structure the world has ever known. Finally, the world will have its beloved leader who will do no wrong in their eyes. Peace and prosperity will easily overshadow any discrepancies that may arise.

With the false prophet in partnership implementing the final control system, a booming global economy will be created so that even the skeptic will have difficulty opposing.

Chapter 10

A NUMBER OR A NAME?

"Him that overcometh will I make a pillar in the temple of my God, and he shall go no more out: and I will write upon him the name of my God, and the name of the city of my God, which is new Jerusalem, which cometh down out of heaven from my God: and I will write upon him my new name" (Revelation 3:12).

I literally trembled when I read these several verses because I realized that the Lord Himself will deal with each of us in a very personal way. It is the Lord who will write His name, the name of the city of God and, *"I will write upon him my new name."* We will be treated with royal dignity after having received our own new name from God.

Satan degrades man to such a level that he loses his name. The names of those following Satan are blotted out of the Book of Life and each person becomes a number.

MEANING OF NAMES

The names given children during biblical times were significant because they revealed something about the bearers' character. For instance, Abram means "high father," but God changed Abram's name to Abraham, meaning a "father of a multitude."

Isaac can be translated with the word "laughter" because his mother, Sarah, laughed when she heard God's message that she would bare a child in her old age.

Jacob translates to the words "deceiver" and "supplanter." When God changed Jacob's name to Israel, the new name reflected the "warrior with God."

The name Moses means "drawn out," which has tremendous significance because Moses was removed from the waters by Pharaoh's daughter.

David's name translates to the word "beloved." David was a man after God's own heart, chosen after Saul's rejection.

TODAY'S NAMES

We no longer give our children names that reflect their character or calling. For example, a woman named Grace isn't necessarily graceful. Likewise, a man named Godfrey doesn't necessarily have peace with God. Names simply identify an individual. When a baby is born, parents choose a name based on their preference and a birth certificate bearing that name is issued.

In these modern times, the spoken name is overruled by the written name. This is evident in dealing with authorities. For instance, we may introduce ourselves by name, but that's not usually sufficient for identification; we must provide a document such as a driver's license or passport to prove who we are. Furthermore, the name on the document has actually become secondary to the number assigned on our passports and other identification.

It may now be a little clearer that the transition from the spoken name to a number can be referred to as an "evolutionary process" of modern times. Whether for good or evil, everyone must participate in this process. Our economic, political, and social infrastructure requires such development; therefore, it is futile to think that we can avoid the dreaded number system prophesied in Revelation 13, a matter that will be highlighted later in this book.

THE NAME OF GOD

"And to Seth, to him also there was born a son; and he called his name Enos: then began men to call upon the name of the LORD" (Genesis 4:26). This is the first time in the Bible where we read that people began to pray by identifying God with a name; however, the Bible does not reveal this name.

Later we read about Abraham who *"...removed from thence unto a mountain on the east of Bethel, and pitched his tent, having Bethel on the west, and Hai on the east: and there he builded an altar unto the LORD, and called upon the name of the LORD"* (Genesis 12:8). Abraham *"...called upon the name of the Lord"* but again, no name is disclosed.

MOSES

After Moses escaped Egypt and found refuge with Jethro, the priest of Midian who later became his father-in-law, Moses met God on Mount Horeb. This remarkable event is described in the third chapter of Exodus. While guiding his sheep, Moses came to Mount Horeb and saw something peculiar; a bush was on fire, but it wasn't consumed by the flames.

Moses, a well-educated man who was certainly courageous, approached the bush to investigate why this was happening. Then we read in verse 4, *"And when the LORD saw that he turned aside to see, God called unto him out of the midst of the bush, and said, Moses, Moses, And he said, Here am I."* God repeated Moses' name twice. Why twice? I believe this has to do with the fact that Moses' name was not changed. It must have been strange for this Hebrew to have an Egyptian name. This prophetically points to the Lord Jesus Christ. The name "Jesus" is foreign-sounding to the Jews. For that reason, many Messianic believers take great pain in calling the Lord by His Hebrew name, "Yeshua."

Moses, the Hebrew with a Gentile name, became Israel's physical savior who led them out of slavery, to the Promised Land, a land flowing with "milk and honey."

God could have used an Israelite who was able to identify with the suffering of the people, someone with whom everyone was familiar, as an honest, upright and courageous man. But that's not what God chose to do. He said to Moses, *"Come now therefore, and I will send thee unto Pharaoh, that thou mayest bring forth my people the children of Israel out of Egypt"* (verse 10).

We must recall that Jesus was not identified with His own people; the rulers of the Jews in Jerusalem, the scribes and the Pharisees and those who tend the temple service. Jesus was this great unknown person, hidden away in Nazareth so that the people would say, *"What good can come out of Nazareth?"*

God used Moses and kept his name in tact to show His people that the salvation He prepared was not of Moses, but of the God of Abraham, Isaac and Jacob.

I AM THAT I AM

How would Moses tell Israel that God had spoken to him? Evidently Moses had already realized that this would be too great an undertaking so he asked God, *"...Behold, when I come unto the children of Israel, and shall say unto them, The God of your fathers hath sent me unto you; and they shall say to me, What is his name? what shall I say unto them?"* (verse 13). How did God respond? *"...I AM THAT I AM...Thus shalt thou say unto the children of Israel, I AM hath sent me unto you"* (verse 14). The words Moses actually heard were *ehyeh-asher-ehyeh* which can also be translated with the words, "I will be what I will be" or "I am who I am." With these simple words God identified Himself as the eternal, unchanging, everlasting One. It's as though He were saying, "Don't try to compare Me to anything else, I am not to be identified with just a name of which there is a multitude among the heathens."

God knew Israel was familiar with the many idols worshipped throughout the land of Egypt but He is the only One, the eternal *ehyeh-I am.*

God did not leave Moses in the dark. He continued to explain, *"...Thus shalt thou say unto the children of Israel, The LORD God of your fathers, the God of Abraham, the God* of Isaac, and the God of Jacob, hath sent me unto you: this is my name for ever, and this is my memorial unto all generations" (verse 15). From a human perspective, we don't really see a name revealed here, but we are being led into an awesome meeting: Man meets God, Moses meets "I Am That I Am."

JEHOVAH GOD

Later, God revealed His name to Moses in the following manner: "...I appeared unto Abraham, unto Isaac, and unto Jacob, by the name of God Almighty, but by my name JEHOVAH was I not known to them" (Exodus 6:3). The name "Jehovah" is most frequently used in the Hebrew Scripture, but the majority of translations simply use the word "Lord."

Regarding the pronunciation of God's name, *Unger's Bible Dictionary* says the following on page 564:

> "The true pronunciation of this name, by which God was known to the Hebrews, has been entirely lost, the Jews themselves scrupulously avoiding every mention of it."

Some Orthodox and Messianic Jews often write the word "Lord" with the letters L-rd or "God" as G-d, so not to make a mistake regarding the name of the eternal holy God. By doing so, they seem to indicate that the name of the Creator is still hidden.

JEHOVAH JIRAH

Added to the name of Jehovah are His actions. For example, when the angel hindered Abraham from sacrificing

Isaac by providing a ram instead, he called the place *Jehovah Jirah*, which means "Jehovah will see" (i.e. provide).

JEHOVAH NIS'SE

When Moses held up his hands in the battle against the Amalekites, the altar he built was named *Jehovah Nis'se* meaning "Jehovah my banner."

JEHOVAH SHALOM

Jehovah Shalom was the name give by Gideon when he built an altar to the Lord who promised deliverance.

JEHOVAH SHAMAH

Jehovah Shamah, which means *"Jehovah is here"* was written by Ezekiel and signified that God had turned to favor the city with prosperity and peace again.

A PERSONAL NAME

During the remarkable event when Jacob wrestled with God for a guarantee of blessing, this unnamed man asked Jacob his name. Why? Didn't the Lord already know His name? Of course He did, but it was necessary for Jacob to identify himself with a confession. Remember, the name Jacob means "deceiver" or "supplanter." He had to confess his name being a deceiver. In response to his confession, we read, *"Thy name shall be called no more Jacob, but Israel: for as a prince hast thou power with God and with men, and hast prevailed"* (Genesis 32:28). That was the birth of the nation of Israel.

Obviously, Jacob knew that it was not just some ordinary man who had wrestled with him. In fact, in verse

30 he confesses, *"...for I have seen God face to face, and my life is preserved."* Jacob knew it was God, and God knew that Jacob was a deceiver. Jacob wrestled until his strength was spent and he could do nothing more but desperately cling to the Living God, *"...I will not let thee go, except thou bless me."*

Not only did Jacob believe in God, but he also knew Him. The Lord had already appeared to him in a dream after he escaped from his brother Esau. During that appearance he received the blessing of Abraham and Isaac, *"...in thee and in thy seed shall all the families of the earth be blessed"* (Genesis 28:14). Jacob was overwhelmed with the Lord's presence but now he takes courage and asks, *"Tell me, I pray thee, thy name."* Who was this man who wrestled with him? Jacob didn't receive an answer but a counter question: *"Wherefore is it that thou dost ask after my name?"*

MANOAH

Another attempt for a revelation of the name that remained secret took place before Samson was conceived. It was Manoah's wife to whom the announcement of Samson's birth was given, *"For, lo, thou shalt conceive, and bear a son; and no razor shall come on his head: for the child shall be a Nazarite unto God from the womb: and he shall begin to deliver Israel out of the hand of the Philistines"* (Judges 13:5). When her husband heard this announcement, he prayed to God for the messenger to return. When he did, Manoah asked the angel of the Lord, *"...What is thy name, that when thy sayings come to pass we may do thee honour?"* (verse 17). As an answer, Manoah received the same counter question as did Jacob: *"Why askest thou thus after my name..."* then he added, *"...seeing it is secret."* The modern English translation of the Hebrew Bible says, *"You must not ask for my name: it is unknowable!"* Later, in approximately 700 B.C., a mysterious man named Agur asked for the name of God and His Son, but confessed, *"Who hath ascended up into heaven, or descended? who hath gathered the wind in his fists? who hath bound the waters in a garment? who hath established all the ends of the earth? what is his name, and what is his son's name, if thou canst tell?"* (Proverbs 30:4).

A HOUSE FOR HIS NAME

Solomon was instructed to build a house for the Lord in Jerusalem. Originally it was David's intention to do so, but because he was a warrior responsible for the shedding of much blood, God did not choose him to build this house, but promised David that his son would, *"...build an house for my name, and I will establish the throne of his kingdom for ever"* (2nd Samuel 7:13). Notice the emphasis that this house was not a physical dwelling place for God, but a place for His name.

When the temple was built and dedicated by Solomon, he solemnly proclaimed its purpose and God's intention to the Israelites: *"...But I have chosen Jerusalem, that my name might be there; and have chosen David to be over my people Israel"* (2nd Chronicles 6:6). Repeatedly throughout this chapter, Solomon emphasized that the purpose of the temple was the presence of the Name of the Lord. Chapter

7:1 documents, *"Now when Solomon had made an end of praying, the fire came down from heaven, and consumed the burnt offering and the sacrifices; and the glory of the LORD filled the house."* This was God's "amen" to Solomon's prayer; His fire came down from heaven and accepted the sacrifices, sealing it with the presence of His glory.

It becomes quite clear that access to God is obtained through His Name. This became evident later in history when the apostle Peter proclaimed, *"Neither is there salvation in any other: for there is none other name under heaven given among men, whereby we must be saved"* (Acts 4:12). That name is Jesus Christ!

"WONDERFUL, COUNSELLOR..."

"For unto us a child is born, unto us a son is given: and the government shall be upon his shoulder: and his name shall be called Wonderful, Counsellor, The mighty God, The everlasting Father, The Prince of Peace" (Isaiah 9:6). Believers know that this child is Jesus of Nazareth, the Christ, the Messiah of Israel and Savior of the world.

We must also consider verse 7 which says, *"Of the increase of his government and peace there shall be no end, upon the throne of David, and upon his kingdom, to order it, and to establish it with judgment and with justice from henceforth even for ever. The zeal of the LORD of hosts will perform this."* Naturally, from an Old Testament Jewish perspective they were waiting for the "prince of peace." They were waiting for judgment and justice on their terms which means that they did not understand God's whole plan of salvation which included the Gentiles.

NAME ABOVE ALL NAMES

"*Therefore the Lord himself shall give you a sign; Behold, a virgin shall conceive, and bear a son, and shall call his name Immanuel*" (Isaiah 7:14). Here we get our first glimpse of the name Emmanuel, which means "God present" or "God with us." The New Testament records, "*And she shall bring forth a son, and thou shalt call his name JESUS: for he shall save his people from their sins. Now all this was done, that it might be fulfilled which was spoken of the Lord by the prophet, saying, Behold, a virgin shall be with child, and shall bring forth a son, and they shall call his name Emmanuel, which being interpreted is, God with us*" (Matthew 1:21–23). The title, "*Emmanuel...God with us*" was revealed in Jesus (Yeshua), which means "Jehovah is salvation." Its unfortunate that virtually all Bible translators have relied on the Greek translation instead of the original Hebrew. The name *Yeshua* or *Joshua* was "Gentilized" and it became known as Jesus in English, a somewhat foreign sounding name to the Jews. However, this doesn't change the fact that by whatever pronunciation or spelling, it still refers to the same person, the Word who became flesh and dwelt among us. He was the One born of the virgin Mary who fulfilled the prophecies of the Old Testament, proclaimed His Messiahship, died on Calvary's cross where He voluntarily poured out His blood in full payment for the sins of all people of all times.

The apostle Peter preached to the Jews in Jerusalem, and we continue to do the same through the written Word: "*Neither is there salvation in any other: for there is none other name under heaven given among men, whereby we must be saved"* (Acts 4:12). The religious authorities in Jerusalem were shocked and immediately forbade the disciples to preach, *"...henceforth to no man in this name."*

Jesus' name is mocked, ridiculed, blasphemed and rejected by an overwhelming majority of the world's population until this very day, yet it is the only Name by which salvation can be obtained.

THE NUMBER

Today's economy, financial system and politics are irreversibly progressing toward a complete numbering system that will eliminate all names. Therefore, it is not surprising that the final totalitarian global system will require that every person on the face of the earth be numbered. Revelation 13:18 reads, *"Here is wisdom. Let him that hath understanding count the number of the beast: for it is the number of a man; and his number is Six hundred threescore and six."* The number of the beast is 666.

At this point, it is necessary to explain that the number system—or any number for that matter—is not evil in and of itself. Some dear brothers and sisters have become upset after receiving a license plate with the numbers 666. They should not be troubled by this; after all, the number 666 follows 665 and precedes 667. There are 66 books in the Bible. The 666th verse in the Old Testament speaks of Abraham's death, *"And these are the days of years of Abraham's life which he lived, a hundred three score and fifteen years."* The 666th verse of the New Testament reveals Jesus' own proclamation of His betrayal and death: *"...Behold, we go up to Jerusalem; and the Son of man shall be betrayed unto the chief priests and unto the scribes, and they shall condemn him to death"* (Matthew 20:18). Such things are coincidental. Seeking a divine meaning in numbers is futile because chapters and verses were not part of the original Hebrew writings, but were added for reference, study and practicality. Nevertheless, the numbering system, now in full swing, will be implemented, and it will be irreversible.

THE NEED FOR NUMBERS

We were faced with a problem coming up with an identity code for our subscribers when the U.S. branch of Midnight Call was founded in 1968. Locating names alphabetically would have been extremely difficult, particularly considering the number of such common names as Johnson. In fact, almost 1300 households bear the name Johnson in our relatively small city of Columbia, South Carolina. Imagine the number of Johnsons in all of South Carolina or the entire United States! So early on in our ministry, we first used zip codes to identify subscribers. This separated the "Johnsons" in geographical areas. Then we added the first and last letters of the family name, followed by the first and last digits of their house number, and the first letter of the street they lived on. We found that such a code was quickly recognized by all our co-workers and prevented virtually all duplications.

There are many different ways to create a code for an individual, but without numbers it is next to impossible. Nothing can stand in the way of progress, which requires that each person on the face of the earth be identified by a number.

IDENTIFICATION NUMBERS

Every person in the United States is issued a nine-digit Social Security number at birth which remains with us until we die. Many more numbers follow: birth certificate, school enrollment, driver's license, and probably a dozen insurance policies and tax numbers for the city, county, state and federal governments. Many laws assure us that the information accessed by these various numbers will be protected from misuse. But what about the future?

We already know the future because the prophetic Word considers the future as history. The documentation of future history clearly reveals that the world will unite as one big happy family pledging their allegiance to one man described in the Bible with the following words: "...*Who opposeth and exalteth himself above all that is called God, or that is worshipped; so that he as God sitteth in the temple of God, shewing himself that he is God*" (2nd Thessalonians 2:4). What will the people do? Revelation 13:8 says that they will worship him, the Antichrist who is Satan in the flesh. He is the masterpiece of the father of lies who presents himself as God and requests the worship of all his subjects.

How is it possible that an informed and intelligent people reach a point where they surrender their dignity, identity, national sovereignty and religion to worship the man whom the Bible refers to as the *"man of sin," "the son of perdition,"* and *"the wicked one"*? We will discuss that in our next chapter.

Chapter 11

THE COMING DIGITAL GOD

"What profiteth the graven image that the maker thereof hath graven it; the molten image, and a teacher of lies, that the maker of his work trusteth therein, to make dumb idols? Woe unto him that saith to the wood, Awake; to the dumb stone, Arise, it shall teach! Behold, it is laid over with gold and silver, and there is no breath at all in the midst of it" (Habakkuk 2:18–19).

"Their idols are silver and gold, the work of men's hands. They have mouths, but they speak not: eyes have they, but they see not: They have ears, but they hear not: noses have they, but they smell not: They have hands, but they handle not: feet have they, but they walk not: neither speak they through their throat. They that make them are like unto them; so is every one that trusteth in them" (Psalm 115:4–8).

When we study these two passages of Scripture, most readers dismiss the notion that an enlightened and educated people would seriously consider trusting a manufactured idol or believe that a man-made object has become divine and deserving of worship. After all, we live in the most sophisticated society in all of human history.

Although a great number of people actually believe that man-made objects can be gods, they are the exception in the Western world. I am sure that it won't be too long before every person on the face of the earth is educated enough to distinguish between what is material and what is divine. So the question remains: What will it take to make an intelligent and educated people worship a man-made product?

HISTORY REVIEW

Man was created approximately 6,000 years ago, and little change was recorded for the first 5,500 when society was primarily based on agriculture and construction. Providing food, clothing and shelter kept man busy. But things began to change in the early fifteenth century. The foundation for the Industrial Revolution was laid with a great number of inventions, including France's introduction of the steam engine in the 1700s; production of electrical currency from a chemical battery in Italy in the 1800s; and Germany's internal combustion engine in 1877. From that point on, man began to replace beasts of burden with manufactured engines which turned out to be far superior for transportation and communication, and became essential for manufacturing.

Before that time, communication depended on the archaic means of carrying letters to their destinations by land or sea. A major milestone was marked when Alexander Graham Bell, a Scottish immigrant to the United States, successfully transferred an audible voice over electrified wire in 1876 in the United States. Less than 20 years later, Italian inventer Guglielmo Marconi unveiled the technology for wireless communication.

What followed has filled tens of thousands of pages documenting the activities of the great army of inventors who have led us to today's modern society.

Today we can instantly communicate with anyone, anywhere in the world. Physical travel to even the farthest destination on earth has been reduced to less than 12 hours.

The "Space Age" was introduced with Russia's launch of Sputnik One on October 4, 1957. On July 20, 1969, man's yearning to dominate space was achieved when astronauts from the United States landed on the moon.

Mankind has seemingly conquered the world, researched every continent, explored every desert, mountain and jungle, and continues to travel into space. Success during the last century has been absolutely phenomenal. Surely the United States' founding fathers would feel like aliens if they were to return to society as it is today.

DIGITAL IDOL?

Anyone over the age of 65 who is reading this book can probably recall their parents and grandparents relaying all types of superstitions which children eventually dismissed as "ol wives tales." But when we go back even further, we find that superstition was not only prevalent in Europe but also in the United States. Anyone who has studied history knows of the witch hunt that took place in Salem, Massachusetts. A great volume of documentation is available and proves that superstitions have ruled the nations for thousands of years. Many superstitious people exist who believe the number 666 possesses a magical sinister power, even if the number appears on a license plate, driver's license, or bank account. But generally, people have become much more educated and enlightened about these matters and are now brushed off more than ever before. Does that really mean people have become enlightened spiritually? No. Because other avenues of deception which thrive on hidden superstitions have now been opened by the great enemy, Satan. Therefore, we must conclude that it is unthinkable for a sophisticated people to believe that they could build a god and worship this man-made object.

However, such a statement opposes what the Bible says. In Revelation 9:20 we read: *"And the rest of the men which were not killed by these plagues yet repented not of the works of their hands, that they should not worship devils, and idols of gold, and silver, and brass, and stone, and of wood: which neither can see, nor hear, nor walk."* This verse clearly reveals that idol worship will continue in spite of all enlightment, education and sophistication.

The preceding verses state that the greatest catastrophe man has ever experienced will occur when the sixth angel sounds his trumpet. Verse 18 confirms, *"By these three was the third part of men killed, by the fire, and by the smoke, and by the brimstone, which issued out of their mouths."* If such is the case, then we must ask again: "How can this happen?" Can intelligent, educated people who enjoy more freedom, prosperity, and luxury than any other time in human history be so blind and ignorant as to worship idols? The question is already answered in Scripture. The answer is yes, man will worship idols.

WHAT IS AN IDOL?

Webster's Dictionary defines the word "idol" as "a deity other than God." In fact, anything that supercedes our affections for the Lord can be considered an idol. Perhaps the strongest force man has at his disposal is faith. It is amazing to see what man can do when he believes in himself or something outside of himself.

How often have we heard the media report about athletes who believed in victory against all odds—and they ultimately achieve that victory?

I am quite fascinated by the biographies of extremely successful people. One thing they all seem to have in common is a goal; they believe in it and dedicate themselves to attaining it.

When the Tower of Babel was built as a way to reach heaven, the Lord defined their work with these words, *"...Behold, the people is one, and they have all one language; and this they begin to do: and now nothing will be restrained from them, which they have imagined to do"* (Genesis 11:6). In order to imagine something, you must have faith; you must believe in the invisible.

Man's downfall began with issues revolving around faith. Eve believed the serpent and Adam believed his wife, but both believed what was contrary to what the Lord had personally told them. The serpent lied to the woman when he said, *"...Ye shall not surely die: For God doth know that in the day ye eat thereof, then your eyes shall be opened, and ye shall be as gods, knowing good and evil"* (Genesis 3:4–5). Of course they believed what God told them, but they also had faith in what the serpent had revealed. This fundamental image placed in man's head by the serpent remains true today: Man wants to be God and will continue to strive toward that goal until he has manufactured his own god the coming digital god.

STUBBORNESS EQUALS IDOLATRY

Idol worship is not limited to man-made objects, but includes his dreams, aspirations and anything else in which he places his faith.

Consider this example in Scripture which exposes disobedience as idolatry: *"...Samuel said, Hath the LORD as great delight in burnt offerings and sacrifices, as in obeying the voice of the LORD? Behold, to obey is better than sacrifice, and to hearken than the fat of rams. For rebellion is as the sin of witchcraft, and stubbornness is as iniquity and idolatry. Because thou hast rejected the word of the LORD, he hath also rejected thee from being king"* (1st Samuel 15:22–23).

Webster's College Dictionary offers five definitions of the word "idol":

1. an image or other material object representing a deity and worshipped as such...
2. (in the Bible) a deity other than God...
3. a person or thing devotedly or excessively admired...
4. a mere image or semblance of something, visible but without substance...
5. a false notion; fallacy...

In other words, an idol is not real; it is built upon a deception, yet man will worship the work of his own hands.

THE ULTIMATE DECEPTION

"And deceiveth them that dwell on the earth by the means of those miracles which he had power to do in the sight of the beast; saying to them that dwell on the earth, that they should make an image to the beast, which had the wound by a sword, and did live. And he had power to give life unto the image of the beast, that the image of the beast should both speak, and cause that as many as would not worship the image of the beast should be killed" (Revelation 13:14–15). The false prophet is the one who instructs those who dwell on the earth that an image of the beast should be built which has life in itself.

The key to understanding this book lies in the word "deception."

THE DECEPTION OF MONEY

The Bible says, *"...the love of money is the root of all evil."* That is a strong statement, but it does convey the value of money. Without it, we can't pay our bills or make any purchases. Everybody, including Midnight Call Ministries, needs money. We could not operate without it. We, too, have to pay wages, insurance, taxes, utilities and multiple other items.

But what is money? Let's look at a dollar bill for example. It is just a printed piece of paper. We can't eat it or fill a gas tank with it, so in and of itself it is useless. The only time money becomes worth something is when it's used as a means of exchange.

Why does that piece of paper have value? The answer is simple: people have faith in printed money. I will not go into the history of money and how it progressed from precious metals to printed paper, but I can assure you that the value we place on our currency is based simply on faith.

This fact is demonstrated in the international currency exchange. The currency of some nations lose value on a daily basis. How is the value determined? On the open market. Investors who believe that a certain currency is a stable investment buy large amounts, hoping that it will increase in value and yield a profit. For example, when large amounts of money are exchanged in US dollars, the value of the dollar increases. Since World War II, the US dollar has enjoyed a relatively stable period and has become the world's leading currency. However, the US dollar is not the strongest currency. Actually, it has lost over 50% of its value against the major European currencies since 1955. But this fact emphasizes that the value we place on currency is based on faith. The entire financial system is built upon an imaginary world with promises of riches in which man must place his faith.

ECONOMIC DECEPTION

Today's economy is built on the free enterprise system. It is important to realize that this free market system is not really free at all. When we start selling, buying or re-selling merchandise, the law requires that we follow strict guidelines established by a number of authorities.

For example, in order to sell a product, we must first

have a retail license compliant with city, county and state ordinances. The licensing requirements increase when dealing between states and becomes even more complicated when dealing on an international level.

Permission from the European Union and the World Trade Organization had to be granted when America's two largest oil companies merged. This practice also holds true for European corporate mergers; the United States must give its approval.

Therefore, "free trade" is only a pipe dream. It is no longer possible because of the interdependency of the nations' economies. Neither the United States, nor any other country for that matter, can make her own commerce law. However, most of us still believe that we work for a free enterprise. That is called economic deception.

FAMILY DECEPTION

For all practical purposes, the traditional family consisting of a husband, wife and children barely exists today. In the past, husbands went to work and at the end of the day, they would return home to their family where a freshly-cooked meal would be ready and waiting. But such families who still practice this tradition are a rare find.

I remember when my children were in school in the late 80s and a social studies teacher asked, "Does your family have dinner together on a regular basis?" Approximately 70% of the students answered "no." Needless to say, times have changed and even fewer families enjoy the tradition of eating a home-cooked meal together.

So we might wonder, "What went wrong?" Actually nothing has gone wrong other than the fact that a progressive destruction of the family is taking place.

Fundamentalists are quick to blame the liberals who support feminist agendas, same-sex marriages and many other extreme left-wing philosophies. Unfortunately, they are only part of the problem. Take a look at Christian families and you will notice the same tendencies toward the dissolution of the traditional family being practiced.

Millions of couples may faithfully attend church, give their tithes and offerings, even support political pro-family agendas, but they are hiding behind the notion that everything is fine while their family is falling apart at the seams.

CHRISTIANS AGAINST THE FAMILY?

Several years ago a very popular Christian talk show host celebrated his ministry's 20th anniversary. In reviewing the wonderful work that the ministry had accomplished over the years, he played a tape of one of the first programs. This is my recollection:

Whenever the family gathered for a meal, everyone was to sit on the chair and place his or her napkin on their lap. Quite naturally, the children failed to follow these instructions. After the parents reminded them several times without success, a new consensus was reached: anyone caught sitting at the table without the napkin on their lap were to go to their bedroom, count to 25 and then return to the table. The audience roared with laughter at the next line, "My wife and I looked rather silly counting to 25 in our bedroom." The lesson was very simple: the parents failed to follow their own rules and the children learned what was expected of them.

On the surface, I thought this was an excellent idea. It was practical psychology. But suddenly it dawned on me that the answer was not as simple as I first thought. What was this minister teaching? Democratic unity of the family. He was teaching egalitarianism, and by doing so he was helping to destroy the God-ordained authority of the parents. That is New Age philosophy strongly endorsed by the spirit of globalism and successfully practiced by Christian psychology.

RULED BY NEW AGE PHILOSOPHY

New Ager's say that all people are equal and there should be no distinction between parents and children. If you think I am exaggerating, take a look at the comic section in your daily newspaper, which we all know serves as a cultural snapshot of a nation. Notice that virtually every comic strip portrays husbands as careless, inconsiderate, self-serving, lazy fools! Why is it necessary to degrade the husbands? The answer is simply because God ordained him as the head of the home. To Eve, God said, *"...he shall rule over thee."* In order to become a pastor, elder or deacon a husband should be *"...One that ruleth well his own house..."* (1st Timothy 3:4). Concerning deacon qualification, the Bible says candidates should *"...[rule] their children and their own houses well"* (1st

Timothy 3:12). Such statements fly in the face of all practical teaching in church and society.

Family deception is in full swing. Who would have dared talk back to a parent only 50 years ago? Who would have questioned a teacher's authority when he punished a rebellious child? Do you see how real family deception is today?

For all practical purposes, it is impossible for modern society to exist without women participating in the labor force. If we followed Scripture's instruction we would be found guilty of discrimination and as a result, we would be violating the law of the country.

To summarize: In order to fully implement the digital god, the world must create a functioning and successful digital society ruled and directed by laws which were previously unheard of.

EQUALITY DECEPTION

"There is neither Jew nor Greek, there is neither bond nor free, there is neither male nor female: for ye are all one in Christ Jesus" (Galatians 3:28). This verse describes true equality. Notice, however, that this egalitarian system is not based on a political philosophy, but a person: *"...ye are all one in Christ."* In order for Satan to implement his digital god, he must imitate this important Scripture to deceive the nations.

In general, what do people want? I believe we can adequately sum this desire up with the words "peace" and "prosperity." It doesn't matter who you are, where you live, or what religious beliefs or political convictions you have; everybody wants peace and prosperity, but on their own terms.

Just before I came into the office to write this chapter I looked at the newspaper. Mort Walker, the creator of the *Beetle Bailey* comic strip showed a soldier writing the following words on a wall: "I see a world where men and women are treated as equals. I see all races, beliefs and cultures cooperating and living in peace. I see a time when we take care of all people who need help and train the ones who don't fit in. I see a blended society with no racial differences or prejudices" (*The State*, 1/7/01). Who in his right mind would object to such a beautiful vision? Do you see how deeply ingrained the spirit of egalitarianism is in the Western world?

INEQUALITY IN THE UNITED STATES

It seems almost hard to believe that women living in the United States didn't even have the right to vote until 1920. During the 2000 election campaign when Al Gore chose Joseph Liebermann as his running mate, the *Los Angeles Times* began its article with the words:

> "When Joseph Liebermann was born in 1942, American Jews still could not buy property in many places in the United States. When he was growing up in Connecticut, Jewish businessmen still couldn't borrow money locally and had to drive into New York City to find friendly bankers. When Liebermann arrived at Yale in the early 1960s, the university still limited the number of Jewish students it accepted" (*The State*, 8/9/00, p.1).

It was only as recent as the sixties that when driving along the countryside we noticed African-Americans parked on the side of the road camped for the night because they were not permitted to stay in a hotel! Our children and grandchildren read about these things in their history class and what do you think goes through their minds? "Old people were so ignorant, so intolerant, so stupid...."

EQUALITY ESSENTIAL FOR SUCCESS

In order to reach a unified consensus with the realization that all people are created equal, each must be educated in egalitarianism. What does that mean? *Webster's Dictionary* defines the word "egalitarianism" as a "belief in human equality, especially with respect to social, political and economic rights and privileges," and a "social philosophy advocating the removal of inequalities among people."

A lot can be said for and against this concept, but as the title of this book indicates, in order for a digital god to take control, equality must be understood theoretically and realized practically.

We have just seen examples of how equal rights were blatantly violated in the United States until just recently. In other countries, the pendulum swings from no equality to a much more advanced equality, as is the case in most European countries. But it is all based on deception because fundamentally speaking there is no such thing as equality. Every single human being on the face of the earth is different. We may have equal rights to a certain degree, but the thought that one can become a true egalitarian is wishful thinking.

Karl Marx, the man accredited as the father of communism, was a great proponent for equality. The apex of communism was exhibited by the Soviet Union in an attempt to incorporate a group of diverse people into one happy family. We all know how it ended; communism went bankrupt and the egalitarian dream died with it, at least it did under the auspices of communism.

HISTORICAL EQUALITY

The dream of equality is clearly expressed in governmental documents all over the world, particularly in Greek and Roman laws.

The United States Declaration of Independence states in part:

> "We hold these truths to be self-evident that all men are created equal, that they are endowed with their Creator, with certain inalienable rights, that among these are life, liberty and the pursuit of happiness."

This statement presumes that all people are indeed equal. What does this equality consist of? It certainly didn't apply to the Indians, the original inhabitants of this country, nor did it apply to the African-Americans who were sold into slavery as easily as meat is sold in a butcher shop. The overwhelming majority of a population of 4 million people in the United States at the time of the Declaration of Independence had virtually no rights. It is also evident that such equality was only designed for the rich landowners and Freemasons who were the leaders of the provisional conquest.

I'm sure that most of us do not like to read such facts and would rather not talk about it, but as Christians, it is necessary to always face the truth no matter how much it hurts. We are destined to walk in truth, it is only the truth that makes us free. I'm not talking about the freedom a government may guarantee—as we have just clearly seen which is open to interpretation—but the freedom which promises, *"...if the Son therefore shall make you free, ye shall be free indeed"* (John 8:36).

EQUALITY IN THE MILITARY

To understand egalitarianism, we must turn our attention to the military. Many countries still have compulsory military service. Young men are ordered to report at military institutions on a given date. Upon identification, the process of integration into an egalitarian system begins. Enlistees are no longer permitted to wear their own clothes; they must wear a uniform. The old Prussian law still stands in most countries: "All must have the same haircut." When they assemble the following day, members of this once-diverse group of people now look alike. But that's only the beginning.

Next comes boot camp where obedience is lesson number one. Individual human dignity is trampled to the ground; recruits have no recourse. In response to orders, they must loudly and clearly respond with the words, "Yes, Sir" and "No, Sir."

This environment accomplishes two things: it abolishes individuality and ensures that all orders are followed strictly, immediately and without reservation.

The soldier loses his personal identity. Even his human dignity is violated. Only the well being of the nation is what counts. He is expected to follow these instructions, even if it means death.

I believe that this example illustrates how the process is in the works now. The whole world will not be serving in the military to become puppets at the bidding of the commanding officer, but all the world is enlisted in another "military force," the forces of darkness. The ruler is the prince of darkness who uses his cunning devices to deceive humanity so that all will become digitized. In other words, people will lose their individuality and become integrated into one gigantic family of nations. They will gladly do the bidding of the leader who finally asks to be worshipped as God.

Egalitarianism is a prerequisite for the New World Order. Our political parties, educational institutions and religious movements all proclaim an imagined reality that all people are equal. It is absolutely necessary that people all over the world merge into a unified pattern because their representatives will act in like manner as is clearly documented in Scripture, *"And the ten horns which thou sawest are ten kings, which have received no kingdom as yet; but receive power as kings one hour with the beast. These have one mind, and shall give their power and strength unto the beast"* (Revelation 17:12–13). The key is that they *"...have one mind"* which is rapidly developing the world over.

Chapter 12

ECONOMIC EQUALITY

O utside of the true equality and perfect unity all believers have in the Lord Jesus Christ, there remains a growing deceptive unity. Scripture says, *"...And that no man might buy or sell, save he that had the mark, or the name of the beast, or the number of his name"* (Revelation 13:17). There will be no more alternative, no more individual rights. People will have only two choices: receive the mark of the beast or die.

From studying the prophetic Word and reading a number of books and articles on the subject, I have concluded that most Christians believe that the Antichrist will install his system by force. People will accept the mark in order to survive. This is only partially true because no one can implement a system without the support of the people. The overwhelming majority of the world's population will wholeheartedly endorse the final system. This is true economically, politically and religiously. During Daniel's time, everyone but Shadrach, Meshach, and Abednego bowed down and worshipped the image Nebuchadnezzar had erected. The words of Revelation 13:3b ring true, *"...and all the world wondered after the beast."* They wondered with amazement, praise and adoration because this amazing man actually produced miracles no one thought were possible.

MARKETING DECEPTION

Deception in the marketing world is based on what people want, and what they will accept. We have become so immune to marketing language that we are unable to distinguish between what is true and what is false. But this marketing deception is not the invention of one clever person; it is the result of how people react to what they hear.

Whom should we believe when we see commercials for the many different car manufacturers and dealers? Every company praises its own product with such conviction that we begin to believe that each one is the very best! Such promotional advertising is not really telling the truth. So the next logical step would be to censor advertising so that only facts can be promoted through the media. If that were the case, we would surely need to double the number of law firms in this country in an attempt to keep up with the impossible task of legislating truth in advertising. Marketing deception continues to prosper by leaps and bounds.

Some time ago, I spoke with several people who subscribed to a food service they claimed was far superior to the grocery store. In one case, I took the time to note all the information and figures, and then compared those figures with what one would spend buying groceries in the local supermarket. The result? The food service charged at least 30% more. Even after seeing my calculations, those who subscribed to this food service were still not convinced! Why not? Because they were taken in by "marketing deception."

VACATION DECEPTION

When our children were small, my wife and I were invited for a hotel promotion in Myrtle Beach, South Carolina. We were promised money for gas and a new computer if we came. Excitedly, we drove down to the beach and went to the hotel. The salesman enthusiastically explained what a tremendous deal was awaiting us. What was the deal? We were guaranteed an annual one-week vacation spot at a certain location. The initial investment would be only $10,000 for that one week reserved especially for us. It didn't take long to realize that this was marketing deception. Without even picking up a calculator, we figured that $10,000 would yield at least $700 a year in interest. During those days, you could rent one of the most luxurious oceanfront apartments for approximately $400 a week. Needless to say, that additional money could be reinvested and after about ten years our capital would have grown to between $13,000 and $18,000 and we could enjoy a week long vacation at one of the best hotels in Myrtle Beach any time we wanted.

But the marketing deception went even further; we found that we were responsible for a housekeeping fee which, at that time, was $68 per week. Our salesperson was rather offended when I told him that his wonderful deal was actually like throwing money out the window. It took some persistence to get our free computer, which turned out to be nothing more than a toy. Yet every year, tens of thousands of people sign contracts and willingly pay above and beyond for their one-week vacation spot.

What fascinates me is that the people who sign these contracts—whether its for a vacation spot, grocery service or any other "fantastic deal"—actually believe that they got a bargain.

From a spiritual aspect, this carries a major message. When we believe even the slightest lie, we are put into the power structure of the coming digital god.

PROSPERITY DECEPTION

"And his power shall be mighty, but not by his own power: and he shall destroy wonderfully, and shall prosper, and practise, and shall destroy the mighty and the holy people. And through his policy also he shall cause craft to prosper in his hand; and he shall magnify himself in his heart, and by peace shall destroy many: he shall also stand up against the Prince of princes; but he shall be broken without hand" (Daniel 8:24–25). Two phrases stand out in particular: *"...destroy wonderfully"* and *"...by peace shall destroy many."* Obviously this man, described as a *"...king of fierce countenance,"* is very successful.

During ancient times, leadership was reserved for the strongest. The one who was able to defeat his competition took up the leadership and it was hoped that he would also defeat his surrounding enemies, thereby enlarging his territorial rule. Actually, this was the case worldwide until 1948 when Israel became a nation again.

The man spoken of in the above passage shall be mighty, *"...but not by his own power."* We know that these words refer to the Antichrist, who will receive his power directly from Satan, as documented in Revelation 13: *"...and the dragon gave him his power, and his seat, and great authority"* (verse 2). How does that happen? Will a man appear somewhere in the world possessing supernatural power and the ability to enforce his authority? Based on what we have learned from Scripture and history, I don't believe that will happen. The Antichrist's rule and system has been in the making since man's creation.

Throughout history, Satan has continued to work his master plan to place all human beings under his authority. That is a known fact for Bible-believers, but how will this come about? Through communication. Since he is the great imitator, he must do as God did and communicate with the people.

How did God communicate? Hebrews 1:1–2 answers, *"GOD, who at sundry times and in divers manners spake in time past unto the fathers by the prophets, Hath in these last days spoken unto us by his Son...."* God reminded us that we have violated His commandments, broken His law and have fallen short of the righteousness He requires of us. Summarizing the message of the Old Testament we can rightly say that man has been found guilty. But then God made a provision in order for man to escape punishment: His Son, the Lord Jesus Christ, who came from heaven in the form of human flesh, died on Calvary's cross, shed His blood, was buried, arose the third day and ascended into heaven.

The New Testament says that *"...whosoever believes in Him shall not perish, but have everlasting life."* So God has made His plan clear: we are guilty, but we can be pardoned. We are law-breakers, but the penalty has already been paid. We are separated from God for all eternity, but we can come to Him through Jesus Christ. The Gospel message is so simple.

But what a terrible product man has made out of the Gospel these days. When we analyze the various religious movements that have somehow attempted to follow the Scripture but have ended up doing their own thing, we find that they have invented their own form of salvation outside the work Jesus already accomplished on Calvary's cross.

Therefore, the Antichrist must present his own plan of salvation to mankind; thus, *"...by peace shall destroy many."*

PEACE DECEPTION?

Most of us would agree that we are living in a time that is more peaceful and prosperous than ever before. The last century saw two world wars in Europe as the center of activity. What were they fighting about? Superiority. Territorial borders were altered during these wars. But as a result, we see that since World War II there has been little territorial dispute throughout Europe, with the exception of the eastern region where people previously living under communism have had to re-adjust to the new global democratic system.

For all practical purposes, it is unthinkable that Spain

would attack Portugal, or Germany would declare war against France. Globalization has made such potential conflict virtually impossible, especially now as the European Union gains ground, political clout and economic power. Any military conflict would be self-defeating.

Wars have not only been fought in Europe, but all over the world. In some cases, particularly Africa, hot spots still ignite here and there. Sooner or later the conflicts will be resolved, agreements will be reached and a negotiated peace will be implemented. Absolutely no nation can afford to go to war or be excluded from the democratic global society. We have seen exactly that with Cuba and North Korea, who have literally been left behind economically in the global race. Other countries such as Libya and Iraq have felt the isolation due to their non-compliance with the laws and regulations of the United Nations.

FREE FROM DECEPTION?

In most countries, free speech and free press are now a reality. During the communist era, free press was exclusively limited to the benefit of the communist system. Anyone could express his view and write whatever he wished as long as it met the guidelines of communist philosophy.

In the Western world, we did not consider communism a free society because our press could write anything, even if it was against the philosophy of our governments. However, during the communist era, the western world developed into an anti-communist bloc so that our free press was only free to express anti-communist philosophy. If a news media would have expressed pro-communist tendencies, the American people would have ignored such media and sooner or later, that firm would file for bankruptcy.

Today, our media can freely criticize anyone for any reason as long as it serves the global criteria to create a better world, cleaner air, purer water, better education and jobs for all people. So, do we really have a free press? With modern communication capabilities, we are able to instantaneously speak with anyone in the world. Whether by telephone or Internet we can reach out to any area of the world. No place is off limits. The world has become open for all to see and hear.

With the fall of Soviet communism, the Western world suddenly found itself without enemies. Now what will all those fantastic journalists write about since the "evil empire" no longer exists? How can you compete against a system that doesn't exist any longer? In the midst of these many bewildering questions have come the AIDS epidemic, global warming, destruction of the rainforest, imminent extinction of the whales and thousands of other issues that have been elevated as global concerns. This new "enemy" has now replaced communism as the number one enemy.

GLOBAL VS. LOCAL NEWS

There's a problem: While at one time our media was limited to the local news and later, news over the wire, today, even a small newspaper, radio or television station has global access and can broadcast news to its audience from literally around the world. Having such a volume of available news and information, the media has to carefully select what people actually want to hear and read. While basic news is regulated by a politically correct global news media, the local media must do everything in its power to keep their subscribers or listeners tuned in. To do so, they must offer the most exciting news, especially the extraordinary or particularly cruel items which always earn top billing.

If a passenger plane goes down, it will make headlines. Should there be a leak in a nuclear power plant, no matter how insignificant, it automatically becomes global news. Terrorist activity is another media favorite. Such news items literally unite the world because everyone knows about it.

So what is media deception? Primarily, it is the transmission of an image that there are great problems all over the world, but the failure to present a true picture of our own hometown, state or nation.

SAFETY IN ISRAEL?

I have led dozens of tours to Israel since 1975. Each time a minor conflict arose, the media reported it in such a way that visiting Israel seemed dangerous. We have always had travelers who cancelled their plans in fear of their safety.

During the Teddy Kollick administration of Jerusalem, a study showed that it was 19 times more dangerous to visit Detroit, Michigan than it was to visit Jerusalem. In spite of the lengthy explanations we tried to convey to the travelers to put their minds at ease, they usually did not change their minds. If they heard the news say that it was dangerous in Israel, then that settled it.

Was the news media telling the truth? Of course. They were reporting the fact that someone had been killed in Jerusalem, but they added that since that was the case, it would be too dangerous to visit. But why do we conveniently forget that at least 70 people are killed daily in the United States by firearms? That's not an exception, but a statistic that holds true 365 days a year.

Murder is no longer reported in the newspaper unless it is local. If someone is murdered in Greenville, South Carolina, which is about 90 miles from our city of Columbia, it will not be printed in our paper. It's considered local news for Greenville and not newsworthy for Columbia. But when something happens in Jerusalem, the whole world hears about it.

Why does the media report such lopsided news? Because they report what the people want to hear. The media addiction is much more serious than most of us will admit. We know the world only based on what the media feeds us; therefore, if an image of a nation can be formed by the media, then why not the whole world? All one has to do is present selected news to create an image in the public's mind.

HURRICANE HUGO

When Hurricane Hugo hit South Carolina in 1989, we watched its progress on the local news. On one broadcast, a young reporter stood on the rain-swept street with microphone in hand reporting some of the damage in the Myrtle Beach area. We all thought it didn't look so bad. This woman was standing in the midst of the hurricane, smiling as she tried to verbalize the extent of damage and danger.

Roughly ten minutes later, the national news, presented by some of the most experienced professionals in broadcasting, came on. Suddenly Hurricane Hugo was portrayed from a very different perspective. It was presented in such a manner that it literally became frightening. Both the local and national news reported the same hurricane in the very same place; however, with their limited funds and talent, the locals could only present an image based on their understanding. The pros presented an image we wanted to see, something extraordinary, exciting and nerve-wracking.

How does this relate to the coming digital god? The news media is either intentionally or unintentionally paving the way to present a universal education so that mankind will learn to think on one level. In the end, freedom of expression and freedom of the press will be limited to the dictates of the image of freedom, based on the definition of a world conscience. That is Satan's intention and in the process, he will *"...destroy wonderfully"* all those who oppose.

The words, *"...destroy wonderfully"* may sound like a contradiction. After all, what's so wonderful about destruction? In simple words I believe this means that anyone who does not comply with the spirit of the endtimes will self-destruct. No force is being used. The news media, for example, who do not participate in the exciting competition in broadcasting has no chance with the viewers and will fall and be destroyed wonderfully.

I must repeatedly stress that this development is not based on a conspiracy of international bankers, the Bilderbergers, the Illuminati, International Freemasonry, the Club of Rome or any other global organization. This deception is taking place because "we the people" are in charge and the consensus of the general population requests such types of deception.

THE O. J. SIMPSON FIASCO

We must recall when all major networks broadcasted the O.J. Simpson trial. The media literally over-reported and people became fed up with the coverage. At least that is what they said during a number of polls conducted during that time. One network temporarily suspended all coverage of the trial. That didn't last but a few hours until it jumped back on the bandwagon because ratings plummeted and they were in danger of losing their audience. Was this a global media conspiracy? Obviously not. Did the news media brainwash the viewers into becoming addicted to their news coverage? Again, obviously not. So who was to blame? Simply "we the people." That's what we wanted and that's what we got!

Chapter 13

ENTERTAINMENT DECEPTION

"For all the Athenians and strangers which were there spent their time in nothing else, but either to tell, or to hear some new thing" (Acts 17:21).

G reece is where democracy finds her roots. The Greek culture is considered to be one of the most refined in all of history. Greek mythology is world famous as confirmed in verse 16: *"Now while Paul waited for them at Athens, his spirit was stirred in him, when he saw the city wholly given to idolatry."* Doesn't this sound like a world capital city of idolatry? They had a god for everything and, as can be seen even today, their craftsmanship was exemplary.

The Greeks were in power before the Romans. They are the third superpower mentioned in the Bible from among the four.

Although Athens was given wholly to idolatry, it was the Grecian language through which the Bible was preserved. Many believe the New Testament was most likely written entirely in the Greek language. Scholars are of different opinions; some insist that the New Testament was written in Hebrew and translated into Greek. The key of contention is that the Greek, in which the oldest Bible manuscripts exist, is a form of language never spoken or used in other Grecian literature. Thus it stands to reason that the New Testament was translated from the Hebrew to Greek. There is no definite proof for this claim, but logically speaking, the book of Hebrews, for example, would not have been written in Greek.

Regardless of these things, it was Athens where people built their own gods and apparently had nothing else to do but debate and discuss news. They wanted to know the "latest" and were hungry for entertainment. This group of Grecians wanted, *"...either to tell or to hear some new things."* No doubt, this was a select group because they *"...spent their time in nothing else."* Somebody had to work, houses had to be built, animals tended, fields plowed and harvested, so this group was obviously not part of the working force; they were the upper class, the intellectuals.

THE FANTASY WORLD

Times have changed. Today, anyone can hear and see a growing selection of entertaining shows, debates, sitcoms and full-length movies 24 hours a day, 365 days a year.

So the question is, "Why go to the movies or spend hours in front of a television set?" Granted there is some educational value in certain programs, but in general, most people participate in these activities simply to be entertained and to kill time of which they claim to have so little.

A great deception is taking place while we are being entertained that most of us are barely aware of. We are being led into a world that just doesn't exist. There is no such thing as Superman, Batman, Touched by an Angel, Cat Woman, Xena the Princess Warrior or the Dark Angel. These, and many other entertaining shows lead viewers away from reality into a whole new world of imagination.

Movie producers learn how to create a visible reality out of the impossible. What is the entertainment industry's intention? Before we answer this question, let me repeat that the entertainment industry only produces films and shows that people want to see.

Through the years I have read numerous commentaries and books written by well-respected evangelical authors who blasted Hollywood and the entertainment industry for promoting immorality, violence and vulgarity over the airwaves. This may well be justified, but the bottom line is still the same: Hollywood only produces what the people want to see.

So what is the goal of the entertainment industry? Well, quite obviously it needs to make money. The members of this industry are in the same boat as anyone else: Everyone has to make money in order to make ends meet, and if possible, make a profit. The more profit is made, the more money is spent for a better qualified staff, the latest high-tech equipment and the most brilliant writers. Only the best engineers, technicians and scientists in the industry can produce the best films.

The second point is competition. In the case of the entertainment industry, if they can't improve your product —which means more brutality, immorality and violence— they lose to the competition and their company will fold.

SINFUL MEN SIN BY NATURE

Man will always follow evil, just as our first parents, Adam and Eve. The Bible actually says, *"The heart is deceitful above all things, and desperately wicked: who can know it?"* (Jeremiah 17:9). In Genesis 6:5 we read, *"And GOD saw that the wickedness of man was great in the earth, and that every imagination of the thoughts of his heart was only evil continually."* Therefore, it stands to reason that man, who is thoroughly corrupt, is unable to produce good. The Bible declares that man is basically wicked. However, today's modern world rejects this claim. So if he does not believe the simple statement of Scripture, he opens himself up to Satan's deception.

You've heard the saying, "There's a little bit of good in everyone." Well, philosophers will glorify the quality of human character. From the field of psychology, we hear that man can be improved, but he must first come to our office for a number of scheduled sessions.

SIN MUST BE PAID FOR

Biblical Christianity differs from all others because while we recognize that we are corrupt, sinful and desperately wicked, we do not claim to possess the capabilities of improving ourselves. Rather, our message is straight from the Bible, *"...Ye must be born again."* This rebirth is based on the fact that our sinful, wicked character must be redeemed. The only price valid and acceptable by the Father for redemption is the shed blood of His Son Jesus Christ. We cannot help ourselves. We cannot hope to become better, but He who says, *"...Behold,*

I make all things new" can transform us from our old corrupt nature into the image of the Beloved.

It is also necessary to add that this is spiritual. Our old flesh-and-blood bodies will continue to be the same. We will battle with the wicked characteristics of our old nature for as long as we live. Pride, arrogance, lying, stealing, adultery and gossip are sins which born again Christians are completely capable of committing, just like anyone else.

CHRISTIAN ENTERTAINMENT DECEPTION

With this we come to the great tragedy within confessing Christianity in relation to our subject of entertainment deception. I am fully aware that it is unpopular to expose this fact because we would rather point out the evil and corrupt liberal system, those who produce pornography, indulge in immorality and flaunt their godless life to the public. But pointing an accusing finger at evil does not help the situation within the Church. The apostle Paul wrote, *"But evil men and seducers shall wax worse and worse, deceiving, and being deceived"* (2nd Timothy 3:13).

In the beginning of chapter 3 Paul writes, *"This know also, that in the last days perilous times shall come"* (verse 1). He goes on to list eighteen characteristics by which we can identify anti-Christianity within the Church. Then he summarizes it with this statement, *"...Having a form of godliness, but denying the power thereof: from such turn away"* (verse 5). This is speaking directly to the Church; we don't need to look at Hollywood to find characters' most fitting traits described.

Our own "Christian" entertainment industry has followed in the footsteps of the world. I am not going to isolate certain groups or denominations that are particularly guilty of promoting the new trend of entertainment because I would surely leave some out and may unjustifiably criticize others. However, Christian entertainment, based on the principles of the great deceiver, is alive and well within the Church.

Some years ago I attended the Spanish Booksellers Convention in Miami, Florida. I was invited to attend a Christian concert during the event. I went with an open mind. There were some good words spoken and some of the music I would consider to be conservative. But as a whole, the entire show heralded confusion. I have no joy in writing this, but objectively, that is what I saw. The performers were dancing on the stage as if demon-possessed, screaming at the top of their lungs so that my ears actually hurt. Before the show was over, I had to get up, leave the auditorium and go to my hotel room. Only after I knelt down, prayed and thanked the Lord for His peace which passes all understanding, did I begin to feel like a normal human being again.

But Christian entertainment is an absolute must if a church, particularly a large one, is to be successful. A Christian bookstore cannot exist without the sale of videos, CDs and cassettes which actually have no biblical teaching value, but are extremely noisy, confusing and damaging to the ear.

Christian entertainment has become a gigantic

industry patterned after the world. It now monopolizes all Christian music and has stepped into the world and presented a "Christian Gospel entertainment industry" to those who have no idea about the Gospel, and cannot distinguish between Christian and worldly music because they have become one.

Chapter 14

IMAGE DECEPTION

"And deceiveth them that dwell on the earth by the means of those miracles which he had power to do in the sight of the beast; saying to them that dwell on the earth, that they should make an image to the beast, which had the wound by a sword, and did live. And he had power to give life unto the image of the beast, that the image of the beast should both speak, and cause that as many as would not worship the image of the beast should be killed" (Revelation 13:14–15).

We already used this passage of Scripture in another chapter, but in view of what we have just learned, I sense it to be important that we revaluate the process of deception. This tendency is reinforced by the fact that when the wrath of the Lamb hits earth, people will be so convinced that Antichrist is right that they will refuse to repent. The Bible says, *"...yet repented not of the works of their hands, that they should not worship devils, and idols of gold, and silver, and brass, and stone, and of wood: which neither can see, nor hear, nor walk: Neither repented they of their murders, nor of their sorceries, nor of their fornication, nor of their thefts"* (Revelation 9:20–21). So Scripture makes it very clear that those who are deceived will wholeheartedly follow the system of Antichrist and defend it until their last breath. For that reason, we must be even more cautious than ever in these last days that deception does not overtake us. After all, Jesus was not making a casual statement when He repeatedly said, *"Take heed that no man deceive you. For many shall come in my name, saying, I am Christ; and shall deceive many"* (Matthew 24:4–5). These few words describe the greatest deception ever.

We previously discussed the fact that the first beast, who is the Antichrist, is a person who has no power by himself; he seems to be just a poor chap who is suddenly propelled into prominence. Everything he has was received directly from the dragon who *"...gave him his power, and his seat, and great authority"* (verse 2). Verse 4, *"And they worshipped the dragon which gave power unto the beast...."* Twice we read in verse 5, *"...was given unto him"* and again in verse 7, *"...it was given unto him to make war with the saints...and power was given him...."*

In contrast, the second beast has authority, *"...he exerciseth all the power of the first beast before him, and causeth the earth and them which dwell therein to worship the first beast, whose deadly wound was healed"* (verse 12). One can't exercise power unless he has power. This power is religiously motivated because through his authority he can cause the entire world, *"...to worship the first beast."*

Instantly our mind races to the preconceived conclusion that power is related to force; in other words, he will force the people of the world to worship the image. But such a conclusion is wrong. The key to unlocking the mystery of this person is "deception." When you deceive someone, you're not forcing someone, you are simply telling them a lie that they will gladly believe.

Many of us who are believers have tried to witness to those who are deceived and each of us has experienced the fact that it is virtually impossible to convince someone that he is being deceived if that person has made a conscious decision to believe the deception.

BELIEVING IN DECEPTION

When Rome was in power, the citizens believed in the system; therefore, the Empire became so mighty that her influence is still felt around the globe even today. Communism also became such a powerful force through the Soviet Union because the people believed that it was the best system and would produce a paradise for workers on earth.

During his short reign, Hitler was successful because the people believed in his ability to defeat all enemies and create a thousand-year kingdom of peace on earth.

Today, virtually the entire world believes that the social-capital-democratic system will bring about peace on earth. There is no opposition to democracy on the political scene. This is also true of economics where free enterprise rules globally.

WORSHIP AND DECEPTION

The word "worship" is actually a strong word when we consider its public definition. All religions worship a god, a deity identified by name and exhibited through pictures, statues, monuments and great buildings or writings. Surely no one would worship a man! That seems to be the logical conclusion, but that's not what it says in the Bible. We repeatedly read that all of the world will worship the beast. How will this take place? Our answer is found in verse 13, *"And he doeth great wonders, so that he maketh fire come down from heaven on the earth in the sight of men...."* What that means is open to speculation. Some of my colleagues believe that the false prophet will control nuclear weapons and at his will, he will be able to make fire come down from heaven to earth. I don't believe that this qualifies as deception because it is real. We must always keep in mind that deception looks real but is not.

In Matthew 24:24 Jesus is speaking of deception when He said, *"For there shall arise false Christs, and false prophets, and shall shew great signs and wonders; insomuch that, if it were possible, they shall deceive the very elect."* Again, *"...great signs and wonders"* are not identified. Therefore, I believe it is of little value to speculate regarding what types of signs and wonders they are, except to say that they are lying signs and wonders, they are false and following him will lead to destruction.

THE IMAGE

What is interesting in this development is that the dragon gives power to the beast. The beast is in possession of power but delegates that power to a man-made image. In the final analysis, it is the image which has the power to *"...cause that as many as would not worship the image of the beast should be killed."*

THE MICROCHIP

How is this possible in practical terms? The Bible says that each person on the face of the earth will receive a mark, either on their right hand or their forehead. This, too, has led to such speculation as a microchip injected in the right hand or forehead. This microchip would contain all personal data such as your name, address, age, health, religion, your bank account number, etc. Those with such a microchip could shop without a billfold or credit card; he would simply walk in the store, select items and walk out. An electronic scanner would detect the selected products and register them. By the time the customer walked out of the store, the computer would have totaled the purchase and deducted that amount from the individual's account. That is a possibility even today.

The skin chip theory sounds plausible, but I do not believe it to be the answer to our puzzle. Why not?

1. The chip under the skin, as has been successfully implemented in animals, is "ancient" as far as computer technology is concerned;

2. The overwhelming majority of people would probably not participate in such action. To insert a foreign object into a person's hand or head is not something people would jump at the opportunity to receive;

3. The under-the-skin chip theory presumes that this technology is the epitome of sophistication. But as I already pointed out, it's old news. By the time you read these lines, the capability of computer science will have been multiplied many times.

TECHNOLOGY EXPLOSION

Each year new technology is placed on the market and outdates and replaces the old one. In our next chapter, we will list some of the progress being made in computer science. Quite frankly, it is phenomenal.

In summary, it doesn't need to be a chip because each person is created in the image of God and is a unique identity, impossible of duplication. There is no one in the world exactly like you or me; we are one of a kind. Today's computers can read our height, weight, eye color, fingerprints, and countless other identifying characteristics. We can be positively identified from among the six billion people on earth. For that reason and many more, we will not speculate as to what the image is exactly. Nor can we speculate as to the nature of the mark which will be necessary for survival during the days of the Antichrist.

ARE WE BEING DECEIVED?

Our chapter is entitled "Image Deception" and we need to look into this matter with a sober mind and ask ourselves, "Are we being deceived?" The answer is absolutely "yes!" Whether we want it or not, or believe it or not, we are being integrated in the process of total deception.

The word "image" is key in these endtimes, particularly since the introduction of movies and television. Each of us forms an image of a subject, product, person or nation. ...Consider this example: The image we have of another country is based on what we have heard, read and seen. However, what we don't realize is that all news is partial and selected based on the criteria of newsworthiness which is based on sensation, the paranormal, excessive cruelty and brutality.

Not too long ago, I went to a class reunion in a little town in Germany called Grefrath. It was the 45th year since graduation and there was much to talk about. From our class of 33 students, three had died and another three lived in foreign countries: one in Spain; another in Brooklyn, New York; and myself in Columbia, South Carolina. I was quite amazed at two questions that seemed to be repeated: 1) Are you going back to America? and 2) Aren't you scared to live there? That was quite a shock to me. I thought I lived in a secure country and I still believe so to this very day. But that's not how they perceived living in America. My concept of America completely contrasted their image of the same country. I must admit that they were much better informed with facts and figures about living in the United States than I was. Nevertheless, these questions clearly showed how an image of a nation is formed.

IMAGE ABOVE ALL

We have already written about the entertainment deception that has transferred the minds of people into a dream world. No one would ever admit it, but the entertainment industry dictates what people buy, how they spend their leisure time and what their dreams are all about.

I was quite surprised when I recently bought a new pair of tennis shoes and noticed that the most popular brands are also the most expensive. After carefully inspecting the tennis shoes, I noticed that there was little, if any, difference in the quality of material or workmanship. Most were made in China, but apparently the brand name was what sold the tennis shoe.

WE GLADLY PAY FOR THE IMAGE

For example, the logo of a brand such as Nike is made visible on the shoe or on any of its apparel; therefore, customers will gladly pay an exorbitant price to advertise this particular brand.

I tried to buy a baseball hat without any logo or brand name and found none. It just goes to show that a person goes to a store and pays extra money so he can promote a company brand. Shouldn't it be the opposite? Advertising is very expensive. Shouldn't the company give a discount to the customer if he advertises their name? This seems extremely illogical to me, yet millions of people proudly run around in their Nike's, Reeboks and other brands, paying additional prices to advertise for these companies. Can you imagine the image of the mark of the beast proudly paraded by six billion people? I can.

HOW NOT TO BUY A CAR

I love to go shopping for a new car, which I do every five to eight years. The first confrontation I have is with the salesperson who usually introduces himself and asks, "Can I help you?" My standard answer is, "No you can't help me. But I can help you make some money if you sell that car to me at the price I want."

Newspaper ads and cleverly created television

programs promise the buyer that he will benefit by coming to a certain dealership. This type of image building is very successful. When the customer has found a car he likes and believes that the salesperson is the one who will "help" him get the car, the battle for the dealership has already been won. The highly-trained salesperson will then prove beyond a shadow of a doubt that the customer is receiving the best possible deal, and that the dealership is barely making any money.

This image of success has been transferred to the mind of the customer who will proudly drive the car home and tell all their friends and neighbors what a great deal he got on this car. Did he really? In most cases, he did not, but he sure did get caught in the web of image building.

THE PRIDE OF THE IMAGE

After I have selected the car I want, I negotiate the price and sign the papers. The salesman shows me the vehicle and explains the function of the car, as he is required by law to do. During the inspection, I noticed that the name of the dealership was prominently displayed on the trunk of the car. I asked whether I would be paid for the promotion I'd be making as I drive all over the Columbia area. This statement obviously caught the salesman completely off guard. Apparently he never heard anyone make such a request. "You mean to tell me that I paid for this car, you make money on the deal and now you expect me to promote your company for free while I drive around town?" I asked. This conflict was taken to the president of the company, who offered to remove the name from the car. Because this would have taken several days, it turned out to be an inconvenience, so I drove off in my new vehicle displaying the name of the dealership.

Of course, the next step would be the maker of the car, another great image for which companies pay hundreds of millions of dollars. For the life of my car I will be prominently displaying the name of the manufacturer and the name of the dealership, as I promote their product and service free of charge. I have become their servant!

It may be understandable when someone buys a used car or one of the cheaper $10-$12,000 models. Such cars don't have an image. They are just a vehicle to get you from point "A" to point "B." It is certainly a different story when you buy a Mercedes because this is a prime brand with an image attached to it, globally recognized as superior. Who would want to ask a Mercedes dealership to remove the 3-pointed star and any trace of the Mercedes identity? Virtually no one, because image is part of the motivating factor to buy this car in the first place.

From that point of view we begin to understand that image deception is very positive, is built upon success, quality, reliability, and everyone will want to be part of this wonderful new world, and in the end, they will proudly display the image of the mark of the beast.

Chapter 15

SCIENTIFIC PROGRESS TOWARD THE DIGITAL GOD

I f I were to summarize our previous chapters in just one paragraph it would be as follows: Mankind exists between two power structures; the holy, righteous and loving God and Satan, the father of lies, who's purpose is to destroy God's creation. In His mercy, God has perfected salvation through the death and resurrection of His Son and He offers it freely to anyone who will believe and receive this gift. On the other hand, the devil does not have the capacity to create; therefore, he must imitate God and offer mankind a substitute. This imitation must be something man can understand and relate to with his five senses; it must be something he can believe in right here and right now. The making of this false god has been in the works for almost 6,000 years, since the fall of man in the Garden of Eden. It will climax with the image of the beast, whom all the world will worship. That is what the coming digital god is all about.

We will not be dealing with the prophetic aspect of the

Bible in this chapter, nor will we attempt to explain Scripture; the purpose of this chapter is to document various relevant news clippings to illustrate that man is very capable of producing the digital god at this very moment!

Machine That Reads Minds Gives Disabled Hope

Scientists have devised a computer that can "read" thoughts and be controlled by brainpower alone. It has already enabled a severely disabled British man to type out a message just by thinking.

The machine's developers now hope that it will eventually enable paralyzed people to type, play computer games and even steer their wheelchairs using mind power.

"This is something really special," said Cathal O'Philbin, a severely disabled man from Walthamstow, north London. "It would make a big difference to me."

O'Philbin, 40, has spinal muscular atrophy, which has progressively taken away his ability to control his arms and legs. His voice is now also deteriorating.

When he tested the "mind-reading" Adaptive Brain Interface (ABI), he found that after three hours' practice he was able to write a message by thought alone; his words were: "Arsenal Football Club."

"The key to our system is its natural and quick operation. Without any assistance, a user can teach the machine to recognize his thoughts within one or two hours," said Jose del Millan, a Spanish computer scientist who coordinated the project at the European commission's Joint Research Center in Ispra, Italy.

The machine's software then "learns" the brainwaves that result and the user learns how to think in a way that makes the machine react. In the session in London last November, O'Philbin was told to think hard about a rotating cube, moving his left arm (which he cannot do physically) and then to relax mentally.

"It was hard work," said O'Philbin, "getting my brain to stimulate the computer to move around the keyboard."

Del Millan said the system might eventually have applications for able-bodied people, but emphasized that his team was not interested in delving into a user's innermost thoughts.

"We are developing applications only where the user consciously decides to issue a command to the computer. We are not exploring the brain at the unconscious level," he said.

—The Sunday Times, 29 April 2001

Professor Set To 'Control' Wife By Cyborg Implant

Surgeons are preparing to create the first husband and wife cyborgs: they intend to implant computer chips in a British professor and his wife to see if they can communicate sensation and movement by thought alone.

The professor hopes it will show how two brains can interact; doctors at Stoke Mandeville hospital, who will perform the surgery, hope it will lead to new treatments for paralysis victims.

The signals from Warwick will be converted to radio waves and transmitted to a computer which will retransmit them to the chip in Irena. Warwick believes that when he moves his own fingers, his brain will also be able to move Irena's.

They may even be able to communicate anger and excitement, because emotions also stimulate nerve activity. "It is like putting a plug into the nervous system," said Warwick.

Ali Jamous, the surgeon who will lead the operation on the

couple, says the technology may one day help people who are paralyzed by spinal cord damage. "The nerves in the leg below the lesion are still working but cannot make contact with the brain," he said. "If we could transmit that signal from one side of the lesion to the other, you could bypass the break."

Ian Pearson, who studies emerging technologies for British Telecom, says several centers are researching cyborgs: "The aim is to control computers and other equipment through direct links to the brain. It is control by thought and I know the military are very interested."

–The Sunday Times, 6 May 2001, P.20

The Measure of Man

"Biometric" technology, which can recognize people from their fingerprints, eyes or other bodily characteristics, is becoming cheaper and more powerful. Is it about to become ubiquitous?

On the Internet, goes the old gag, nobody knows you're a dog. The usual way to prove who you are when picking up e-mail, shopping online or visiting a closed area of a website is to type in a password—a surprisingly old-fashioned form of security that would be recognizable to a Roman soldier. But though passwords are simple, they are far from secure. Many people use the same one for everything. Worse, they may use a common word such as "hello," their phone number or their dog's name—any of which could be guessed by an intruder.

Which is why some people champion a more high-tech approach. Rather than using a password to identify yourself to a computer, why not use a physical characteristic such as your voice, face or fingerprint? Such bodily measures, known as biometrics, have the appeal that they cannot be lost, forgotten or passed from one person to another, and they are very hard to forge. Proponents of biometric technology imagine a world in which you sign on to your office computer using a fingerprint scanner, take money from a cash machine that scans your eye to ensure you are the account holder, identify yourself to your bank over the telephone via a voiceprint, and check in for flights by walking past an airport camera that identifies you as a frequent traveler.

Being digital

Biometrics come in many forms. The idea is said to date back to ancient Egypt, when records of distinguishing features and bodily measurements were used to make sure that people were who they claimed to be. Modern computer-based biometric systems are employed for two basic functions. The first is identification ("who is this person?"), in which a subject's identity is determined by comparing a measured biometric against a database of stored records—a one-to-many comparison. The second is verification ("is this person who they claim to be?"), which makes a one-to-one comparison between a measured biometric and one known to come from a particular person.

Fingerprints are the most widely used biometric. Ink-based fingerprints have been in use for over a century, but in recent years they have gone

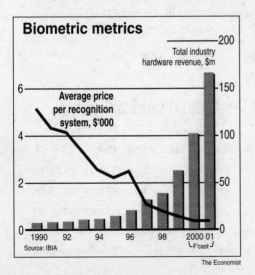

Biometric metrics

Total industry hardware revenue, $m

Average price per recognition system, $'000

1990 92 94 96 98 2000 01

F'cast

Source: IBIA

The Economist

digital. Modern electronic systems distill the arches, loops and whirls of conventional fingerprints into a numerical code. This can be compared with a database in seconds and with an extraordinary degree of accuracy. Fingerprints have the advantage of being cheaper and simpler than most other biometrics, and account for around 40% of the market.

Another popular biometric is hand geometry.

Hand-geometry systems are already used to control access and verify identities at many airports, offices, factories, schools, hospitals, nuclear-power plants and high-security government buildings. They are also used in "time and attendance" systems, in which shift workers clock on and off using their handprints—preventing time-card fraud through "buddy punching." The best known example of the technology is the INSPASS program, which allows frequent travelers to the United States to skip immigration queues at seven big airports by swiping a card and placing their hand on a scanner. Recognition Systems of Campbell, California, which supplies the scanners for the INSPASS program, says that over 35,000 of them are in use around the world.

—The Economist, 9 September 2000, P.119

Rx: Plenty Of Bed Rest And A Gold Microchip

Engineers tackle new ways to take medicine.

Imagine: a brief doctor's office visit, a quick poke, and a gold chip inserted safely beneath the skin. With the chip gradually releasing medicine, a diabetic might go months or even years without an insulin injection. A cancer patient could break free of intravenous tubes tethering her to a machine. Children with ear infections would delight in abandoning foul-tasting antibiotics.

The microchip is at the forefront of a remarkable revolution in drug technology, one that combines improbable materials like gold and plastic with a host of medications. Crafted by Robert Langer and his colleagues at the Massachusetts Institute of Technology, the gold chip is one of several novel approaches being used to outwit "problem" drugs—those that must be injected frequently, for example, or that have serious side effects. Langer's work has also spawned a new field of science, pooling the expertise of chemists, engineers, and biologists to produce novel systems for delivering drugs.

Though the gold chip remains untested in humans, and is too small in its present form to painlessly deliver insulin (a $3 billion market), it may provide a solution for many other drugs. Like a mini gas station, the chip incorporates hundreds of drug-containing reservoirs. Implanted under the skin or, potentially, swallowed, it delivers medication via electric pulses generated by the chip itself or by a handheld remote.

Such cutting-edge technologies are less futuristic than they sound. Langer's implantable drugs already benefit thousands of patients with brain cancer. The brain is notoriously hard to medicate because of the blood-brain barrier, tight junctions between cells that protect the brain from toxins and microbes—and also bar therapeutic drugs.

More drug-delivery inventions are on the way, if the number of people designing them is any indication. "Ten years ago...people looked at us a little strangely," says Edith Mathiowitz, an engineer inspired to improve drug delivery during a postdoctoral fellowship in Langer's lab. Now, training young "bioengineers" at Brown University, Mathiowitz marvels that a field born just a few decades ago has successfully merged the worlds of machine and molecule in a way that not even Langer would have imagined.

–U.S. News & World Report, 5 July 1999, P.55

Sci-fi Vision Of The Bionic Human Takes A Giant Step Forward

The bionic man could soon be more than just a figment of science fiction.

British scientists have developed a substance that could join humans to machines.

Up to now it has been difficult to connect the body's complex biological system with sophisticated electronics. But the new material, a kind of porous silicon, is capable of being turned into electronic circuitry, say its makers.

It will mean human tissue such as nerves and muscle fiber could be grown on micro-processor chips, leading to true "bionic" limb replacements.

At the moment, replacement limbs are often slow and clumsy and do not come anywhere near being able to copy the delicate and intricate movements of a natural hand or arm. The material, developed at De Montfort University in Leicester, could also lead to the development of electronic sensing devices for checking the body.

Fully-biocompatible silicon microprocessors could one day even be used to replace brain tissue damaged by injury or by diseases such as Parkinson's or Alzheimer's.

Professor Sue Bayliss, from De Montfort, said: "The ability to culture cells directly on to porous silicon offers exciting possibilities for the future."

–The Express, 6 April 1999, P.18

High-Tech Clothes

"Super" clothes fight odor and bacteria.

Innovative techniques in clothing manufacture offer garments that actively keep you safe and comfortable: jackets that grow warmer when the temperature drops, sweat socks that resist bacteria and odors, and T-shirts that ward off ultraviolet rays and might one day kill mosquitoes on contact. Such "super" clothing could soon become widespread, French technologists believe.

Many of these new clothes make use of microcapsules: tiny, spherical membranes bound to the clothing fibers and containing beneficial substances. The Damart company makes a "thermo-regulating" jacket coated with microcapsules on the inside. The capsules contain a substance that stores heat energy by melting at normal temperatures, and then releases that energy by crystallizing as the temperature falls.

Many scented and odor-resistant clothes contain microcapsules that release a perfume or odor-neutralizing chemical when the fabric is rubbed. The Neyret company offers a line of scented lingerie that employs this technology. Another firm, Francital, will offer a line of deodorizing underwear in 2002. (A prototype of such underwear was worn by two explorers for 45 straight days during an expedition to the North Pole).

–*The Futurist*, Jan/Feb 2000, P.12

Growing Chips

While computer scientists are developing ways to replace silicon chips, researchers at Purdue University have found a way to extend silicon's usefulness by making chips smaller and faster. The key is to layer the silicon transistors to make three-dimensional integrated circuits.

Conventional computer chips have one layer of two-dimensional silicon transistors. The new chips use transistors that are one-fiftieth the size of a human blood cell. These chips automatically "grow" silicon islands on each layer of the chip upward to form additional layers. Because the layers of transistors are stacked, connections between them are shorter and circuits are closer together than with conventional chips. That results in higher performance, lower power dissipation, and lower costs.

To "grow" the layers, holes are etched into silicon dioxide and filled with silicon. Embedding a single-gate transistor in the oxide layer and etching holes down to the silicon lets the silicon grow up through the holes and across the transistor to form a second layer of transistors. Those transistors carry twice the data of existing transistors.

–Popular Science, November 1999, P.45

Technology On A Tiny Level Is The Next Big Thing In Science

After years on the fringes of science and engineering, nanotechnology—the manipulation of individual atoms and molecules—is moving to center stage. Supporters say its effect may be greater than the sweeping changes driven by the computer industry over the last half-century.

"Nanotechnology will lead to the next industrial revolution," the White House Office of Science and Technology Policy proclaims in a report subtitled, "Shaping the World Atom by Atom."

The possibilities to create new things appear limitless," said Horst Stormer, a Nobel Prize-winning physicist at Lucent Technologies in

Murray Hill, N.J. "Nanotechnology has given us the tools to play with the ultimate toy box of nature—atoms and molecules."

Some examples from the White House report:

Paint made of nanoscale pigments that automatically changes color to match its surroundings. A chameleon airplane, mimicking the color of the sky, would, in effect, be invisible to the eye.

Bricks that sense weather conditions and alter their molecular structure to modify the transfer of heat or humidity. They would increase your comfort while lowering your energy bill.

Molecular sensors to detect poison gases, chemical leaks, spoiled meat or the first stirring of cancer cells.

Computer chips so tiny you could put "a Pentium on a pinhead," said William Warren of the Defense Advanced Research Projects Agency, which was instrumental in creating the Internet.

American private industry is spending a comparable amount; Europe and Asia, twice as much.

In the nanoworld, objects are measured in nanometers —1 billionth of a meter (a meter equals 39 1/2 inches). That's about four times wider than an atom and 10,000 times narrower than a human hair.

"Weird things happen," said Robert Mehalso, a researcher at Rensselaer Polytechnic Institute in Troy, N.Y. "The old rules of physics don't apply."

The full effect of nanotechnology will be greater than just computer chips because it applies to many more fields than electronics, the federal report said. "Nanotechnology has the potential to change the nature of almost every human-made object," the report says.

"These nanotubes are incredible," said Richard Smalley, a chemist at Rice University in Houston and a Nobel Prize winner. "They are expected to produce fibers 100 times stronger than steel at only one-sixth the weight—almost certainly the strongest fibers that will ever be made out of anything."

One intriguing use of nanotubes is to store hydrogen—an inexhaustible, nonpolluting fuel—in cars and trucks. Theoretically, a tankful could last 2,000 miles.

"It's your future fuel tank," said Richard Truly, director of the National Renewable Energy Laboratory in Golden, Colorado.

—*The Kansas City Star,* 6 February 2000, P.A4

Scientists Are Scanning The Brain For Traces Of Guilty Knowledge

On July 22, 1977, the body of retired police Captain John Schweer lay bleeding on a railroad track in Council Bluffs, Iowa. Blame for the murder fell on teenager Terry Harrington, who has spent over two decades in a state penitentiary protesting his innocence. Now Harrington says he finally has proof that exonerates him. A new technology called "brain fingerprinting" suggests that Harrington's brain doesn't contain memories of the crime scene, but it does recognize specific details about the concert he says he attended on that fateful night.

Reading someone's memories through a helmet of electrodes sounds like science fiction. But surprisingly, scientists say they can do just that. The Harrington case is the first time lawyers have ever submitted such brain measurements to a U.S. court, and within days a judge will either reject them as "junk science" or accept them as evidence that could help reopen Harrington's case.

Many researchers hope they can do better than polygraphs by targeting the source of the lie: the brain. The "brain fingerprinting" technique used on Harrington was developed by Lawrence Farwell, a scientist and businessman at Brain Wave Science in Fairfield, Iowa. Farwell's technique exploits a signal that the brain emits when it perceives something familiar.

If a person watches random numbers flash on a screen, for example, the brain will suddenly show a distinctive electrical response called the P300 if personal information like a home phone number pops up. Scientists have known about the P300 response for decades, but no one has tried to apply it in a real-world criminal situation. Farwell believes it is valid in the Harrington case because he found details about the crime and Harrington's alibi that weren't in court transcripts or newspapers. For example, the murderer escaped by running behind a building through waist-high weeds and grass. According to Farwell, the real murderer would remember tearing through this thick underbrush. But when Farwell showed Harrington a photo of the building, the convict said he didn't know what lay behind it. And when presented with words such as "cement and blacktop," "sand and gravel," and "weeds and grass," Harrington had no special brain response to the correct answer.

Someday, investigators could check to see if a suspect knows other criminals or victims by tracking eye movements. That's because the brain scans familiar faces differently than it does strangers' faces. Another way of getting into the brain might be to look at response times. Travis Seymour, a cognitive psychologist at the University of Michigan —Ann Arbor, has studied how quickly people can press buttons while being shown information on a computer screen. When presented with words and images that they either know or don't know, he has found it takes people longer to press a "don't recognize" button when they're lying—nearly twice as long as when they truly do or don't know.

–U.S. News & World Report, 15 January 2001, P.40

Improved GPS System Will Be Available To All

Until now, civilians using a U.S.-built network of satellites for navigation got a less accurate reading than the military out of fear that potential enemies could use the system to shoot at missiles.

Police, firemen, emergency crews will now be able to respond more accurately to exactly where help is needed.

The change will make satellite navigation devices people already own 10 times more accurate, Lane said, and will not require the purchase of new machines.

The difference will mean satellite navigation can be used to track a missing person to an area about the size of a tennis court. Until now, the area of intense search would have been more like a football field.

The system, known as GPS, is used by more than 4 million people worldwide for everything from navigating in traffic to oil exploration. Boaters and hikers use hand-held GPS devices, and similar equipment is now installed in wristwatches and in the dashboards of some cars.

–The Kansas City Star, 2 May 2000, P.A2

Speech-Enabled Design

Think3's Chairman and CEO Joe Costello wants to simplify the way that industrial and mechanical designers and engineers interact with CAD/CAM software. He wants them to gain the ease of use and higher productivity possible with a speech-enabled graphical user interface. When using speech command and control, the user's eyes and hands are free to concentrate on the graphics area, instead of swapping focus between the graphics area and the interface. The idea is to free engineers to innovate, rather than battle the software, says analyst Charles Foundyller, president, Daratech Inc., Cambridge, Massachusetts. In addition to bringing high-end 3-D functionality to the desktop, think3 version 6.0 uses games-based learning software to bring novices up to speed with 3-D design skills. For more information: www.think3.com.

—Industry Week, 15 January 2001, P.5

Smart Food For Robots

Sandro Mussa-Ivaldi, a neuroscientist at Northwestern University Medical Center, has created a robot with the brains of a fish. Not impressed? Consider how he did it: He wired a two-wheeled robot directly into a lamprey's brain stem.

To control the robot, Mussa-Ivaldi co-opted the part of the lamprey's brain that normally works to keep the fish's body balanced. Light receptors on the robot sense the surroundings; then a computer translates that information into electrical impulses, which are fed into the lamprey's neurons. They interpret the impulses as they would if they were trying to keep the fish swimming upright. The computer then translates the cells' signals back into electrical commands instructing the robot how to turn its wheels in response to a light. Neuroscientist Miguel Nicolelis at Duke University and his colleagues have achieved similar success with owl monkeys. A computer program reads electrical patterns in the monkeys' brains and uses them to move robotic arms—one right in the lab, another 600 miles away at MIT, connected via the Internet— exactly as the animals moved their real limbs.

Such work could eventually lead to prosthetics that move naturally and provide tactile information. Nicolelis thinks it might be possible to train the human brain to control entirely novel robotic body parts if they are appropriately wired into our neurons. "You could directly control a robot on Mars and obtain feedback about the texture of the surface the robot is touching," he says.

–Discover, February 2001, P.16

Trial Program Uses Digital Fingerprints To Speed Lunch Line

The tiny ridges on a student's index finger could soon make school lunch money and lunch-line bullies a thing of the past.

A fingerprint identification program used in three Pennsylvania school districts allows pupils to pay for chicken nuggets, sloppy Joes, pizza and other cafeteria delicacies without carrying cash.

Students place their index fingers on small scanners, and a template matches them with their electronic prints. The program plots 27 points on a grid corresponding with the fingerprint's ridges.

The fingerprint image is discarded, and the points are assigned numbers. The system's manufacturer says that only the numbers are retained, and those cannot be reinterpreted into a fingerprint image.

The American Civil Liberties Union, however, fears that the technology—known as biometrics—could hasten the end of privacy rights. Biometrics uses unalterable physical characteristics to verify a person's identity.

"It's a sign of things to come," said Barry Steinhardt, associate director of the ACLU. "We will be able to be identified with biometrics in virtually every situation. The use of the digital fingerprint is just one example of that."

Biometric devices that identify people by physical

characteristics— such as eye patterns, voice tones and hand prints—
have been the stuff of cinema for decades. Until recently, cost had
restricted their use mainly to government offices and military bases.

Within a year, however, mobile phones and personal computers
will have fingerprint scanners as optional equipment, providing
convenience as well as increased security.

A new experimental system that lets middle-school students pay
for their lunch through fingerprint identification has raised privacy
concerns. The technology, known as biometrics, is also used to
identify criminals, but the manufacturers of the cafeteria payment
system maintain that it cannot be applied to forensic use. Here's how
it works:

The Associated Press

The student places her index finger on a scanning device
that takes a digital image of the fingerprint. The image is
then resized and standardized, which is not the case in
the technology's forensic application.

The system 27 points on a grid that correspond with the fingerprint's
ridges. The image of the fingerprint is then discarded, and the points are
assigned numeric values unique to the student. According to the
manufacturers, the system retains only the numbers, which cannot be
reinterpreted into an image of the fingerprint.

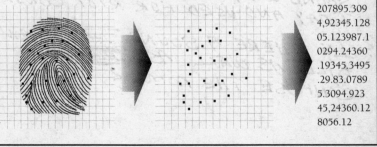

207895.309
4,92345.128
05.123987.1
0294.24360
.19345.3495
.29.83.0789
5.3094.923
45,24360.12
8056.12

Source: Sagem Morpho Inc.

–*The Kansas City Star,* 28 January 2001, P.A6

CONCLUSION

We must emphasize that all news relating to technology becomes old news the moment it is reported. Development on the technological level is literally mind-boggling; what's new today may be obsolete tomorrow. One thing becomes clear, man is desperately trying to achieve the ultimate creation: artificial life! In the end, man will succeed in building this image reported in Revelation 13:15, *"And he had power to give life unto the image of the beast, that the image of the beast should both speak, and cause that as many as would not worship the image of the beast should be killed."* It is much later than we may think!

IN the beginning GOD SAID...
HE (GOD) SPOKE AND IT WAS
DONE; HE COMMANDED AND IT
STOOD FAST. (GENESIS 1:3; Ps. 33:9)
SOUND IS ENERGY. SPEAKING IS
SOUND.

SOUND WEAPONS ARE AVAILABLE IN ISRA
TODAY AND USED FOR RIOT CONTROL.

? IS THERE A SOUND THAT CAN
KILL AS WELL AS ~~[illegible]~~
CONFUSE THE MIND?

Chapter 16

THE MAKING OF THE IMAGE

AN INTERVIEW WITH JERRY P. BROWN

Mr. Brown is Manager of Information Services for the South Carolina Department of Labor Licensing and Regulations. He and his wife Susan live in Columbia, South Carolina and have four children. Mr. Brown is a former Navy pilot and expert in computer communication.

The following 21 questions and answers serve to shed additional light on the mysterious image of the beast, the mark of the beast and the number of his name.

THE ULTIMATE CONTROL

Revelation 13:14–17 documents the following: "...*And deceiveth them that dwell on the earth by the means of those miracles which he had power to do in the sight of the beast; saying to them that dwell on the earth* (people), *that they should make* (manufacture, produce) *an image to the beast, which had the wound by a sword, and did live. And he* (the false prophet) *had power to give life* (only God gives life) *unto the image of the beast, that the image of the beast should both speak, and cause that as many as would not worship the image of the beast should be killed. And he causeth all, both small and great, rich and poor, free and bond, to receive a mark in their right hand, or in their foreheads: And that no man might buy or sell, save he that had the mark, or the name of the beast, or the number of his name."*

Q: The ultimate global society will be controlled by a man-made image. This man-made image must be related to a computer because a computer is today's authority in data control, identification and numerous other important functions. If this image is able to recognize who is worshipping it, we must answer an important question: Is artificial intelligence possible?

A: The answer to that question depends on your definition of "artificial intelligence." If "intelligence" means that a computer can make decisions based on its own input, and base these determinations on its past findings, then the answer is "yes." In other words, if a machine can "learn" from past mistakes, and won't make those mistakes again, some people would classify that as intelligence. That means it's a thinking, targeting thing. Making the leap between that type of intelligence and becoming self-aware by saying, "I know I'm intelligent" is quite a jump and one that I don't see happening in the near future. I'm not sure that in my lifetime a computer will become so intelligent that it considers itself a being and understands what it does.

Q: Are you saying it is impossible after your "lifetime"?

A: I don't believe that anything is impossible anymore after watching everything that has transpired within the last ten years. On the other hand, setting up a computer's learning curve so that it learns by action is happening today and it's happening commercially. Advanced implementation of this logic, called "fuzzy logic" is found in industrial robotics worldwide. I know they're doing it at MIT and Stanford. A certain level of computerized intelligence exists. That's a given. Computers already control the markets. You don't control the markets; I don't control the markets. Not even the stockbrokers control the markets. The markets are actually controlled by the systems in the middle that initiate and consummate the orders. The brokers can initiate orders, but the stock markets themselves had to put in some curbs on computer trading in the past. The computers are following their own programs of stock trends. They are automatically buying and selling large blocks of stock at computer speeds without any human input and that was one major reason why the stock market was knocked back several years ago.

Q: At this point in time, with the exception of sharing information, can one computer learn something from another one? And if so, how?

A: Downloading is the key. When you put a pile of bolts and chips together, you basically have a dumb computer. You download to that computer to make it smart. Think of your desktop computer running the Windows operating system. That was really downloaded from another computer. It may be on a CD when it gets there but it's still logic that was created elsewhere that you put in your computer. It makes your system accurate to a certain degree, so it runs on the same program the other computer is running. Before this process began, your computer was literally dumb; it only had the capability of receiving "knowledge," but after the download of the new software your computer has suddenly become "smart."

Q: Does that mean I can continue to implant more knowledge into my computer and outsmart you?

A: I suppose now is the time to talk more specifically about "artificial intelligence." Are machines smart? I don't know about you, but I am constantly corrected by calculators and spell checkers. Does that make the computer smart? No. Can it outsmart me? You bet! Is it smarter than I am? It's not even close. I can download massive amounts of specific "smarts" into my PC. It plays chess much better than I can ever hope to, or rather, it goes through the moves better than I do. But my computer does NOT play. It has no consciousness. I can program my computer to print out "I AM CONSCIOUS"; I can even program it to argue that it is conscious, but it is at best a simulation.

Computers "think" by manipulating ones and zeros. But, the ones and zeros by themselves have no meaning. They only have the meaning we attach to them.

Let me explain it another way. The computer knows nothing of what it is doing. It just shuffles ones and zeros. At it's roots, a computer is just a pile of electronic circuits rapidly changing voltage levels. It calculates mathematical problems, but it knows nothing about math.

I am smarter than my son's hamster. My son's hamster is smarter than any computer I have ever worked with.

Every computer I have ever worked with can out-perform me in whatever it is programmed to do. But it cannot "outsmart" the hamster. Until the computer can outsmart my son's pet, I will not consider it "artificially intelligent." Perhaps it can only be described as a "simulated thinker."

Q: What took place in 1987 when Wall Street experienced a near meltdown?

A: That was an issue where the computers were actually responsible in a sense. Once you turn them loose, you don't have to touch them; they can make their own decisions concerning stock trades. Today, computer trading blocs are limited; they are put under controlled limitations. But the thing is, computers are now deciding the limits as to what their programs are able to do. So stock trades are consummated at the computer level; they are no longer consummated by pen and pencil. A legal pad and pencil is not the final authority that tells me I own a certain stock; it's now an electronic computer record.

Q: Let's talk about identity. I noticed that in recent years when traveling overseas or entering the United States, the immigration officer no longer considers your passport the final authority in determining your identity. The passport must be authorized by a computer.

A: I dare say that recognition of passports will be obsolete in a few years. It is not conceptionally difficult to see the elimination of passports or other forms of identification. The replacement method of identification will involve retinal scans, DNA samples and fingerprints.

For example, you should be able to go to any port of entry in the world to have them do a retinal scan. There's only one retina that looks like mine in the world. From what I understand, you can tell that's me going through that gate, and it couldn't be anybody but me, because it would be virtually impossible to replicate my retina in anybody else's eye. So, in that case, why would I need a passport when traveling from country to country? Once they look at my eye and say "you are Jerry Brown from South Carolina," you have positive identification in place. That's taking the technology to the next level and it is technically feasible to do that today. I see it almost as a certainty.

Q: Let's say I purchased a ticket from a legitimate travel agency. I go to the airport, present it to the ticket counter and the agent recognizes it as a proper ticket. But then he finds it's not on the computer. Will I get on the plane?

A: The computer has to recognize it as a legitimate ticket; it doesn't matter whether or not the agent recognizes it as such. If the barcode is corrupted or something happens so that the computer can't read it, then they would have to manually key it in the computer to verify whether or not it is a valid ticket. So even if you buy a ticket and pay for it at a travel agency, if the airline's computer spits it out, saying "this doesn't match my protocol," then you no longer have a ticket, and most likely, you will not get a seat on the plane.

In modern industry we find people stepping back and not being involved anymore. They're letting the computer do its thing. The computer does it much more efficiently, much more cost effectively, much more accurately; that's just the way it is today.

Q: Joel [Froese] mentioned something not too long ago about a computer being able to read your brain waves. Scientists have tested it in some universities. One person went into a test room not saying anything, only thinking: Lights on! The brain waves recognition system measured the waves and activated the light.

A: Yes, such research is currently taking place. I've seen these studies on the Discovery Channel and have occasionally read about them in periodicals. Your brain works in certain patterns and certain areas of your brain activate when you think certain thoughts. So theoretically at this point in time, you can tell whether someone is lying, or whether someone wants a certain action to start or stop by watching these large levels of activity in their brain. You can also identify intent to defraud, or a particular person knows he's doing wrong. But there's a big difference between that and checking on somebody's thoughts, like what a particular person thinks of me, or what she's thinking about now, or what he'll be doing on vacation next year. That is so far beyond the scope of the current research. We are not there. It's still fiction.

Q: But can't you see that "fiction" being turned into a fact sometime in the future?

A: Sure, there are a lot of people who do this kind of work that are a whole lot smarter than I am. They are doing things that I have no idea about today, but based on what I understand, and have heard and read, they're not there and it will be quite awhile before they get there. However, steps are being taken in recognizing micro-thought patterns. Determining between thoughts such as "yes" or "no" and "on" or "off" are much easier to tell. It's one state of being or another. However, when you start thinking in shades of gray, or you start dealing with memory, then you find yourself confronted with a whole new beast. I don't understand how they would even begin to go about that today, but if someone is sitting in this chair a hundred or even 50 years from now, he will tell a different story. It's outside my realm of knowledge.

Q: Am I right to assume that it does not necessarily mean it depends on one person, one scientist or one computer engineer, but it is a collective knowledge that is being built?

A: The reason the technological explosion is happening so rapidly is because one person cannot build a rocket that flies to Mars, one person cannot build a nuclear plant, one person can't possibly hold the thoughts in his head. So the major technical revolution of the 20th century has been the result of the ability to collaborate knowledge into one entity so that engineers, architects, nuclear physicists and office managers can work from a common core of knowledge.

It's like a nuclear physicist who doesn't know how to lay concrete. They may not know anything about the operation of a computer or the control panel, but he knows what the reactor has to do. The scientist knows the content of the fuel, the alloys that have to go into the reactor, the control, the fuel rods, etc. In nuclear engineering, they specialize even farther where one person works with the fuel technology and another works on reactor design. They have to share knowledge. It's not one person building a nuclear reactor; it's not one person building anything anymore if it requires more than just putting things together and saying "Look, I made a bookcase."

To do anything technical—such as building a computer—requires legions of people. The technology is shared across national boundaries and travels electronically at the speed of light. So it's just a major pouring and sharing of knowledge at this point.

Q: Let's revisit the passage of Scripture we read at the beginning of this interview: This machine the Bible refers to as *"...the image of the beast"* will be able to detect whether or not you are worshipping it. In reality, doesn't the lie detector test already do this today?

A: Yes, it's achievable, maybe even today. Ultimately, it could delve into intent and evasive thoughts. Today, if you took a lie detector test, even using the best technology available, there is still a margin of error. If they ask whether you are a believer and you say you are when you really aren't, the detector may think you are, so you have passed the test. If you say "yes" and the detector thinks you're lying, you've failed. There is a level of uncertainty in the current state-of-the-art lie detectors, which is why they are not technically admissible as hard evidence; they are circumstantial. I can almost guarantee that somewhere down the line a 100% absolute lie detector—such as DNA testing—will be available. You may not even need to ask questions; perhaps a daily surveillance of your activity will enable it to come to a virtually perfect conclusion. That's a little more subtle, but I dare say that maybe within my lifetime, certainly within the lifetime of my kids, a computer with some sort of logic system in place will be able to determine sentiment and loyalty pretty accurately, maybe absolutely accurately.

Q: In regard to the legal system, a good lawyer spends a lot of time researching cases similar to the one he is working on. Let's say, for example a woman has killed her husband. The couple had two children and maintained an average income. The lawyer must find cases where this had happened before in order to effectively defend her. This is very costly and time consuming. If all previous cases were put into the computer, they would be instantly available. Could this technology be used effectively within the mechanics of the process of law? The defense lawyer and the prosecutor could make full use of such statistics to the benefit of all parties, leaving judgment based primarily on the computer.

A: In a way this system already exists. Legal precedents are searchable across the Internet. You can purchase a CD that has every case ever filed in any state. I know you can buy a full-court CD package from the state of South Carolina and do a search on case names, case numbers, case subjects, and case titles. For example, to try and find whether there are any precedents about annexing a shopping center for the sake of tax revenues. These precedents already exist. They are available to be searched at computer speed today. Even the average lawyer or, anyone for that matter, can sit down and take the legal precedent CD's and run a test against this classification and come up with every decision made in the last hundred years concerning that rule of law. Even now lawyers bring convincing arguments in court based on laws and rules of precedents.

Q: Now let your imagination continue: Can you see a state prosecutor and defense lawyer standing in front of a computer to present their case? Could the computer analyze the case better than the judge or jury? We know that a jury can be inaccurate. In general it works, but we have had cases where innocent people have been put in jail, while others were found innocent when evidence clearly proved they were guilty.

A: Two issues must be overcome. One is the technological issue and we're probably close to overcoming the technology issue of that scenario. Second, however, is the social issue. Theoretically, if you read the Constitution, for that to occur, one of the three branches of government, the judicial branch, would have to abdicate its power as people. To allow machinery to make decisions, right now, would probably be considered unconstitutional. You would have to fundamentally alter your definition of a judge and doing so would literally be considered an act of social revolution. I don't think anybody's willing to do that today.

Q: Granted, it may be unthinkable today, but that can change. Keep in mind that most of our parents didn't have running water or electricity, but our children are "at home" with electronic gadgets that were unthinkable to our parents.

A: We don't even have people who can accurately predict the stock market from one day to the next; how can you predict the future relating to judicial matters? However, when people become more comfortable with technology, such as those who are born and raised in this age of global computerization, they may very well think, "that would be cool, we can let the machine make decisions based on black and white and not based on emotion or subjective reasoning." Computers are very objective, not subjective. But a social revolution would literally need to take place in this country in order for that to come to pass. It may not happen in this country first. Who knows? Maybe it will happen in Europe.

Q: Let's talk in global terms. Our subject is global control based on the Scriptures' statement, *"...and deceiveth them that dwell on the earth."*

A: Of course it would have to be done in one area first. In other words, something of that nature, that magnitude, would not squeeze the globe into one. All nations cannot decide they want to abdicate to a computerized judge, and the power of the United Nations is not to that point today. It would have to take place locally first. Some country would have to make the first move, and if it worked, it would be globally accepted. When you think about it, whoever makes the first move might just be in the position to control it. So you have to consider that as well. But today it's somewhere in the future. Socially, I just don't think mankind is ready to do that yet.

Q: How will the new generation behave when it reaches adulthood?

A: That's easy. I believe it will act just the same as our generation if we had been born 30 years later. People are fundamentally the same since the days of Genesis. Try to imagine how you would personally adapt if you had been born into this technology instead of vacuum-tube radios. People adapt to the situation at hand. They have the same drives and impulses you and I had when we were kids. Consider what we have grown used to. In the past 50 years we have voluntarily given up control of some of our actions to the guidance of simple machines. Think of the traffic light. You don't make the decision to stop or go, but that computerized light does; therefore, it controls the gas pedal and the brakes on your car. If our generation so willingly gave up some freedoms to the control of machines, to the greater good, why would we think our children wouldn't also?

Q: Speaking of change, will America accept the metric system?

A: Metrics work extremely well; the whole world uses the metric system with the exception of the United States. The United States just flat out will not change because inches and pounds have worked for years and Americans were born into it. So there's always going to be some resistance, but ultimately, this country will become metric. Sooner or later it has to because we cannot indefinitely remain the island of non-metric measurements. Certain ideas take over more quickly than others. The stoplights controlling intersections make too much sense for it not to be. Not only is it cost effective, but it also extends the life of the policeman by not having to direct traffic from the middle of the road!

Q: Electronic identity is so promising; no more driver's licenses, Social Security cards or other important items to worry about, thereby eliminating fraud and crime.

A: That technology exists today. You could make an economic case for doing that at a supermarket checkout line within the next few years. It's there, it's proven, it works. But it's one of the social issues where people are going to have to be willing to surrender a little piece of their individuality. So it, too, may take a while. The older generation is dying off, and the young kids today are not so intimidated. To them it's not so foreign. My parents were raised on depression-era farms behind a mule. To them, the farthest thing from their mind would be go to a checkout and be approved by a retinal scan. Neither one of my parents have ever even used an ATM.

Q: For all practical purposes, computer development is virtually unlimited. Or is there a limit?

A: I believe that everyone has come to the conclusion that things that were considered impossible ten years ago are sitting on a desktop today. Giga-FLOP technology, that's a billion floating point instructions every second; one billion monetary calculations in less time than taking a breath. That's just a tremendous amount of computing power. Computer technicians twenty years ago said we would never get there. However, now you can buy those computers for under $2,000 and have them on your desktop. That kind of computing power was unthinkable just ten years ago. Nobody is saying there is a limit, never rule out the future.

Q: Are today's computers powerful enough to hold conversations, or to translate from one language to another as you speak?

A: Almost! Today's computing power is smart enough to do speech recognition, although the software is a little spotty; however, the hardware is easily capable of it. It's all in how the programming is done to make it more accurate. It requires too much of a learning curve by the computer owner to understand your account versus mine. So if your desktop takes your dictation based on your accent, its not going to work when it gets to my side because I speak differently than you do.

The Tower of Babel is being rebuilt. But instead of using bricks and mortar we are using silicon.

In a very short time, you will be able to wake and say, "Computer, tell me the weather in Berlin and send a note to Uncle Helmut wishing him a Happy Birthday in German."

Q: Do you see a computer having the ability to

recognize everybody in the world? What needs to be done?

A: You simply have to build its database with the points you want to compare, whether they are fingerprint or retinal patterns. All you have to do is collect the data points and store them in a computer. It can then compare these points much more quickly than any human ever could.

My thanks to Jerry Brown for answering these 21 questions relating to computer science. We have now learned that computer science technology is growing at an explosive rate and that no one can really predict the end. However, Bible-believers know what is to come. Prophecy predicts that the world will unite in order to create the fulfillment of Scripture almost 2,000 years ago, *"And all that dwell upon the earth shall worship him..."* (Revelation 13:8). This was absolutely impossible only 50 years ago, but is an unquestionable reality today. The world, as it is today, already has the opportunity to direct its worship to the image of the beast via computer technology. It is later than we may think and that should make every Christian rejoice because Jesus is coming soon!

Chapter 17

A BRIEF HISTORY OF ELECTRONIC COMMUNICATIONS
BY JOEL FROESE

Joel Froese is the System Manager of Midnight Call Ministry. He entered the computer field in the mid-80s and has accummulated considerable knowledge and experience through various computer-related projects with Midnight Call Ministry. Presently, Joel is studying Computer Science at the University of South Carolina. I have asked Joel to write this chapter, giving us a brief history of computers in layman's terms.

–Arno Froese

For thousands of years electricity was the domain of only a few experimenters. Their knowledge of it was very limited and dealt only with static electricity; however, the 1800's brought about decisive changes in the understanding and application of electricity.

First, you need a source of electricity, and at the very beginning of the century Alessandro Volta invented the battery. In 1821 Michael Faraday built the first crude electric motor and later in 1831 a usable dynamo (generator.) Now a mill could be removed some distance from its power source by using a generator (usually falling water or steam) and motors on the actual machines. And even before Thomas Edison, arc lights bathed cities in a bright blue-white light much like an arc-welder.

However, the seminal event in communications occurred in 1836 when Samuel F. B. Morse invented the telegraph and, of course, the Morse code. Charles Pezold eloquently explains the significance of this event in his recent book entitled, *Code*:

> The instantaneous worldwide communication we've become accustomed to is a relatively recent development. In the early 1800s, you could communicate instantly and you could communicate over long distances, but you couldn't do both at the same time. Instantaneous communication was limited to as far as your voice could carry (no amplification available) or as far as the eye could see (aided perhaps by a telescope). Communication over longer distances by letter took time and involved horses, trains, or ships.

This was obviously a turning point in communications. Wires were soon strung across many countries and under the oceans connecting the entire industrialized world. In the 1890's, Guglielmo Marconi developed the radio, which now allowed communication between places where wires were not practical or even possible, such as a moving ship. So by the end of the 19th century, information could race around the world at nearly the speed of light.

Ensuing inventions allowed a person's voice to be carried over these same wires (telephone) and also on radio waves. This made electronic communications more accessible to the general public; they were interacting directly with the technology now, the intervening telegraph operator was no longer necessary.

Radio, in turn brought about the new concept of broadcast, which is the direct communication of one person to many. Previously, to hear a speech or musical performance you had to be part of an assembly usually in some kind of auditorium at some specific place. This was limiting in several ways, the most obvious being geographically; in other words, you had to be there. In the case of a speech, you could read about it in the newspaper the next day, but the written word does not have the same intimacy. Furthermore, it was exclusive, even if there was no cost involved, there was always a particular segment of the population that would not be welcome at certain events due to race, class status, or other reasons. Financial barriers prevented attendance both by cost of the event and travel.

Radio changed all of this. Now a president could address an entire nation of citizens scattered across a vast country...live. Entertainers, formerly classified as "starving artists," could become rich and famous if catering to the popular culture (radio probably created the concept of 'pop culture') of a nearly limitless audience.

Despite the technical complexity of sending a moving picture over radio waves, television was an inevitable progression from radio. However, it made an even greater impact on society. It is a more intimate medium; a television viewer feels more involved (although he is not) watching a program on TV rather than just listening to a disembodied voice over the radio. When radio programs were "converted" to television, these differences were soon discovered and exploited.

In the half-century since it's invention, we can see that that television has not just affected our culture, but has actually driven it. Although it probably began with radio, television is a relentless force in erasing regional dialects and homogenizing culture.

ENTER THE COMPUTER

Although this may seem like an entirely different subject, we will soon see how the computer generally ties into television and media. It used to be that computers were thought of as amassing and processing data, but now in the age of the Internet, the connection to communications is obvious.

Computers actually pre-date the practical uses of electricity. Blaise Pascal built a totally mechanical computer back in the 17th century. However, the first practical computers really came into existence in the beginning of the 20th century, but only for very specific tasks such as processing census data, calculating artillery trajectories, and code breaking. Gradually large businesses realized the benefits computers had to offer in data processing and accounting. Due to their size and cost, computers remained a rare sight.

The first electrical computers such as the Harvard Mark I (1943) and Mark II were actually electro-mechanical, meaning they were filled with clattering relays. The next innovation was using vacuum tubes, such as in University of Pennsylvania's ENIAC (1945) and John von Neumann's EDVAC. These machines were much faster, but created a lot of heat; consequently, vacuum tubes had a tendency to burn out randomly.

The watershed event in the history of computers began with an invention at Bell Telephone Laboratories in 1947. A remarkable device known as the transistor did everything a vacuum tube could do, but was a fraction of the size and used much less power. Therefore this device generated much less heat which meant it didn't burn out like vacuum tubes tended to do at the most inopportune times. This brought about the pocket-sized transistor radio and the miniturization of all types of audio equipment. More importantly, it marked the beginning of the computer revolution.

Not only were these transistors much smaller than vacuum tubes and relays, but several transistors could be carved out of one piece of semiconductor, creating an "integrated circuit" (IC). Eventually, technology was refined in order to allow thousands of individual transistors to be carved out, wired together and packaged in what is now known as a "chip." These, of course, are the building blocks of a modern computer, and the manufacturing technology keeps advancing every year; today, chips contain millions of transistors!

While transistors decreased the size of the computer from room-sized to refrigerator-size and eventually a desktop box, they remained tools of government and large businesses and were used for very specific purposes. The next revolution took place in the early 1980's with the development of the personal computer. Because they were built on an open standard, soon there were numerous manufacturers building "IBM-compatible" personal computers. Since they were compatible, they could all run the same programs and use nearly all of the same accessories. This was important because now software developers could write a program once that would run all IBM-compatible personal computers. This was not previously possible because almost every mainframe and mini-computer was programmed differently. Now, with a larger than ever user-base, thousands of firms (and individuals) create tens or even hundreds of thousands of commercial applications. This finally made the computer a versatile, multi-purpose machine.

The greatest innovation of the 1990's was the Internet. Although its predecessor, ARPANET, was developed in the late 1960's, and other consumer on-line services as well as business-oriented networks existed, the sheer magnitude of the Internet quickly dwarfed all other communication networks beside the telephone system. Now computers all around the world having access to this infrastructure can browse websites of millions of companies and individuals and send e-mail to any location at no additional cost. This became very popular because of improvements in modem technology and faster computers. However, the Internet really took off when the web browser was invented and the HTML standard was approved in 1990 at the CERN Research Institute in Switzerland. Prior to this development, the Internet was harder to use and generally offered only text as opposed to pictures (although it was always possible).

Website and email addresses have become so ubiquitous that they are advertised with the assumption that everyone has access to these resources at home, work, school, or at least a local library. Generally this is already true throughout the industrialized world, and interestingly enough, many of these newer technologies such as the Internet and cell phones are being adopted at an even faster rate in third-world countries where phone service has historically lagged behind. It seems like everybody in the world wants to be part of this communication revolution!

While radio introduced us to the revolutionary concept of broadcasting (one to many communication), the Internet has expanded the number of "broadcasters" to include anyone with the time, ability, and interest to create a website; thus creating "narrow-casting." Although there is no guarantee people will take an interest in your website, the fact that it is available to anyone in the world with access to the Internet is certainly revolutionary! The ability of an individual or small organization to create a professional-looking, full-color brochure or print advertising is typically cost-prohibitive, but on the Internet anyone with a little ingenuity can create a presentation that is on par with any large corporation.

The Internet is actually just an infrastructure, and the web and email are applications that rely on it. Real-time voice conversations and even video-conferencing can be transmitted over this infrastructure, but only a few early-adopters are using it right now because the technology is still somewhat primitive. However, this is the general direction that electronic communications is taking: convergence. Computers, telephones, televisions, and other "information appliances" will eventually be hooked to one network that delivers text (e-mail), voice (telephone), and video (video-conferencing, broadcast, and pay-per-view movies). Coupled with advances in mobile technology, you will have access to any information you want regardless of where you are geographically located. While this may sound like advertising hype, you may be asking yourself, "Why would I want any of this?" It certainly is the wave of the future, and we have already seen the beginning of it in the 1990's.

The point of this whole discussion is to show how all forms of telecommunication will eventually rely on computers. Even the standard, reliable telephone will be replaced by a sophisticated multi-use terminal even if the user believes he does not need any of the new functions. Of course he then begins to rely on these new functions and wonders how he ever got along without them. For example, all new digital cell phones have caller-ID; there is no extra charge for this service since it is an integral part of the technology. You might believe that you don't need this extra frill, but soon you will appreciate knowing who is calling before you answer.

"In whom the god of this world hath blinded the minds of them which believe not, lest the light of the glorious gospel of Christ, who is the image of God, should shine unto them...For God, who commanded the light to shine out of darkness, hath shined in our hearts, to give the light of the knowledge of the glory of God in the face of Jesus Christ. But we have this treasure in earthen vessels, that the excellency of the power may be of God, and not of us...We having the same spirit of faith, according as it is written, I believed, and therefore have I spoken; we also believe, and therefore speak...While we look not at the things which are seen, but at the things which are not seen: for the things which are seen are temporal; but the things which are not seen are eternal" (2nd Corinthians 4:4,6–7,13,18).

The motive behind writing this book is the revelation of the truth of the Gospel. In contrast to this truth is the lie of the enemy, the *"...god of this world"* who *"...hath blinded the minds of them which believe not...."* This revealing statement shows that the entire world lies in darkness as far as the knowledge of God is concerned. The exception is clearly mentioned in this passage of Scripture: the believers who have received the knowledge of the glory of God. That means we believe in something that doesn't exist as far as visible reality is concerned. We believe that God is the Creator of heaven and earth, He sent His Son Jesus Christ to die on Calvary's cross in our place, and He paid the full penalty for all who believe. As a result, each believer becomes enlightened by means of the Holy Spirit and begins to recognize truths that are hidden from the rest of the world.

The last verse we quoted is significant because it states that as believers we have our sight, not on the visible things of this world; rather, we walk, act, believe and strive toward things which are not seen but are eternal. Therefore, the things we have written about in this book may not be understood by those whose minds are blinded and do not believe.

The documenation we have set forth throughout this book leaves no question that deception is a belief in something that is not real, yet exists on all levels in our modern society.

We also explained that this deception, which is particularly evident in the entertainment industry, is not forced upon the population, but in reality it seems the world actually wants to be deceived.

We highlighted these facts in our discussion of business deception, particularly in the field of advertising. It was also a fact made clear in our discussion of the news media. We saw that the media is not guided by a conspiracy to brainwash the population; rather the people actually dictate the news. This was made especially clear with the O.J. Simpson trial. Television viewers determined and requested that the network continue to broadcast even the most minute details of this sad and often comical event.

I have attempted to highlight many other things we confront on a daily basis to show that the coming great deception is not in the far distant future, but is a reality today.

THE COMING DIGITAL GOD

While the coming digital god is still a subject in the future, we may rightly argue that it is simultaneously already present. We can only buy and sell through the digital system implemented in modern society. The products we wish to buy or sell is controlled through various digital systems.

For example, you can't go to a store, pick up a shirt, pay with printed money and just leave. That is a thing of the past. All the information about this shirt is stored in a digital bank and can only be accessed by certain digital equipment. The sale will only proceed after the cashier scans the digital barcode, translates the code into dollars and cents, and then transfers the ownership of that shirt upon payment, which in most cases is rendered with a digitized credit card. Only then are we proud owners of a new shirt.

Just a few decades ago, no one would have known where that shirt went, who bought it, or any information about the customer. Usually a carbon copy sales receipt was all the documentation necessary for the buyer and seller. In our digital age, the store has shoppers' names, addresses, credit card numbers and much more information that we most likely would not care to know the company has accummulated about us. Moreover, this information is not stored in a file cabinet in some warehouse facility to be kept for a certain number of years; it is permanently stored in a computer. This computer is not hidden in some basement as company property, but is accessible by various means, particularly through the worldwide Internet. The computer knows who we are, what we bought, how much we paid for each item, and much more. That information can virtually be kept for a lifetime.

WHO AND WHAT IS THE DIGITAL GOD?

At this time, it is a system capable of receiving and dispersing information about anyone living on planet Earth. The global master file is a reality today. Based on such available information, the system will continue to develop in accordance with the wishes of the people. Because the people are deceived, or as we read in the beginning, their minds are blinded by the god of this world, they will willingly and even deliberately support this wonderful global system which has brought more peace and prosperity to the world than ever before.

Just think for a moment about what would happen to criminals. They wouldn't get very far because the digital system will be able to identify all activity as well as the movements of every individual on earth. Who in his right mind would refuse such a wonderful system that eliminates crime?

Finally, the governments of the world will balance their budget because everyone will have to pay taxes as required by law. At this point, we have an underground economy that some experts estimate to be 20% of the entire economy. Therefore, hundreds of billions of dollars are written off each year as uncollectible because the global digital system is not fully implemented on all levels of our society.

In summary, the coming digital god is expressed by total control. That is the aim of the evil one who attempts to imitate God. He wants to be the creator, the great god, the glorious redeemer of mankind, but he achieves it through deception, not by truth or by light, but by darkness.

HOW ARE WE TO ACT AS CHRISTIANS?

Serious Christians are asking this question more and more frequently during these endtimes. My answer is that we do not have to act or react to this development, but live in truth before the Living God who has purchased us with the blood of His own Son, the Lord Jesus Christ.

As believers, we make full use of all technology available to us in this world. The apostle Paul tells the believer, "...*all things are your's*..." (1st Corinthians 3:21). But there is a clear and definite distinction between "them" and "us," "they" are in darkness; "we" are in the light. "They" are in the world and of the world, "we" are in the world but not of it. Our goal is to radiate the truth of the Gospel to people everywhere and by doing so, we hope and pray that those who are still in darkness find the liberating light of Him who said *"...I am the light of the world."* True believers walk by faith, not by sight, and they can exclaim with Paul, *"...we are confident, I say, and willing rather to be absent from the body, and to be present with the Lord"* (2nd Corinthians 5:8).

The digital god is coming with all cleverness and sleight-of-hand, offering peace, happiness and prosperity to all who will follow him. As believers, we know that there is no lasting peace, happiness and prosperity outside of the Lord Jesus Christ.

ANTICHRIST

The epitome of the coming digital god will be revealed through a person whom the Bible calls the Antichrist, the man of sin and the son of perdition. In 2nd Thessalonians 2:4 his true intention is exposed: *"...who opposeth and exalteth himself above all that is God, or that is worshipped; so that he as God sitteth in the temple of God, shewing himself that he is God."* How is that possible? In the same chapter it further explains, *"...Even him, whose coming is after the working of Satan with all power and signs and lying wonders, And with all deceivableness of unrighteousness in them that perish; because they received not the love of the truth, that they might be saved"* (verses 9–10). This is the key: *"...signs and lying wonders...deceivableness."*

We have outlined in this book according to various deceptions and repeatedly emphasized that people generally choose the lie instead of truth, darkness instead of light.

Verse 11 continues, *"And for this cause God shall send them strong delusion, that they should believe a lie."* God puts His eternal seal upon these people by confirming their deception and sending them a *"...strong delusion, that they should believe a lie."* That is the great tragedy of the endtimes. People from all walks of life can still be saved; each one can come individually to Jesus and receive forgiveness and eternal life, but many deliberately and continuously choose darkness over light as stated in John 1:5, *"And the light shineth in darkness; and the darkness comprehended it not."*

In view of these facts, the apostle Paul concludes this chapter with these words, *"Therefore, brethren, stand fast, and hold the traditions which ye have been taught, whether by word, or our epistle. Now our Lord Jesus Christ himself, and God, even our Father, which hath loved us, and hath given us everlasting consolation and good hope through grace, Comfort your hearts, and stablish you in every good word and work"* (verse 15–17).